Contents

So, what exactly is this book about?

The book contains 16 stories of teddy bears with mental health issues and each has three components to it. First there is the story, then an update several months or years later, and a final part entitled '*And another thing…*', which gives information that will hopefully be helpful to the reader should the issue resonate with them.

Disclaimer

Although illustrated with teddy bear photographs, this book contains some adult material and is aimed strictly at grown-ups.

Some of my stories are loosely based on real people who either suggested I write about their issue or they have given me permission to write the story in the hope that its content could help others. All names and identifying details have been changed to protect the privacy of these individuals.

In most of the other stories, names, characters, businesses, places, events and incidents are either the product of my imagination or have been used in a fictitious way.

Any resemblance to actual persons, living or dead, or actual events is purely coincidental.

A Word of Thanks.

Writing this book has been possible through a very heart-warming coming together of many individuals. When I told people about my book and why I want to write it I was met with kindness, love, prayers, professional advice and lots of help and support.

- Martyn Hett, my younger son who tweeted about me and got the press interested. Martyn also proof read and edited some parts of the book.
- Louise Murray, my second youngest daughter who set up my DEPOP shop long before the book came into fruition.
- Nikita Murray, my youngest daughter who helped me parcel the teddy bears and hearts, sending them all over the world.
- Dan Hett, my oldest son who helped me publish the book. I don't do technology.

- Nicky Demirci, who proof-read my stories and made my English much better sounding. English is not my first language and she knew what I meant to say and put some things in much better English than I could ever have dreamt to do.
- Joanna Saatchi, one of my longest standing and closest friends who not only wrote the foreword for this book but also kindly proof-read the And Another Thing... sections in each story. Without her encouragement this book would never have got started.
- Alison McQuade, who insisted I do a couple of Christmas Fairs with her to sell my hearts and teddy bears.
- Helen Rose, who checked over and added to my topic on Vicarious Trauma as I did not want to miss something important.
- Gill Dunkerley, who checked over and added to my topic on Stress. Her Mindfulness knowledge is fabulous and I quoted what she told me about it.
- Barbara Rosenthal, who discussed with me the issue on bereavement and helped me add valuable points. Bereavement is her specialist topic.
- Dr Stuart Murray, my husband. Thank you for taking some of the bears for more unusual photo shoots at the surgery.
- DEPOP for enabling me to sell the teddies to lovely people all over the world.
- The Post Office in Heaton Moor. Thank you to Jamie Hulbert, his sister Emma Hulbert, Julie Leather, Anita Woodfinden and Nicky Kirwan.
- Luke Richards who took amazing photographs of my bears

The Knitters

To enable me to continue writing the book many people came forward to help me with the knitting of the teddy bear components to enable me to assemble them more quickly and give them their distinctive features. Thank you, you enabled me to whizz through my many requests for teddy bears.

Binnur Pala (main knitter – she told me she puts a little prayer in each stitch and feels privileged to be a part of this story), Victoria Taylor (very avid knitter for me and gets so many teddies out of one ball of wool – unbelievable!), Collette Uddin (seeing my despair and dilemma about the many bear orders and my need to write the book, yet not having enough hours in the day to do both she suggested I ask for help with knitting), Joanna Saatchi, Jane Hogan, Gill Dunkerley, Pam Drysdale, Dr. Jacqueline Chang, Angela Walton, Andrea Browne, Mary Nelson, Wendy Murray (my delightful mother-in-law), Hattie Woods, Hannah Collings, Louise Murray (one of my daughters) and Emma Milnes (another one of my daughters). Thank you also to Barbara Hodskinson who tried to arrange more knitters for me.

People Who Joined In

I have had some amazing encounters with people from all over the world. Some were incredibly touching, others were very funny. This journey has enabled me to connect with people from many different countries. My customers come from all over the UK, the United States of America, Sweden, Germany, Austria, Italy, Brazil, Chile, Hawaii, Canada and Slovenia.

I don't take myself too seriously and when selling my teddies I decided that I wanted my customers to connect with their own not quite so serious side. So I always send each teddy off with a little story and ask my customers to let me know how their teddies have settled in.

- There is Steve, a truck driver from the States who bought Barnaby. Barnaby got lost on the way and Steve was wondering if "he had stopped in NYC for a little holiday or maybe he was eating Eli's cheesecake in Chicago". So because poor Steve had no bear I made him Barnaby Junior who arrived safely and I was sent a photo of the little fellow sitting on his dashboard. I was delighted. Then I got a message a couple of months later to say that Barnaby Senior arrived after all. So Steve is the proud owner of two Barnabys and Steve and I had a few nice conversations about the meaning of life in general.
- John was sent to a lovely guy in Canada and I was told that he was adapting to life in Canada with a Tim Horton's coffee!
- I was told that Alvin "arrived safely in sunny Texas, safe and sound!
- Ronnie and Evelyn "arrived in the US safe and sound. They are busy getting used to their new home.."
- Hayley has "settled in overseas and is now enjoying her new role as a lady of leisure".
- One lady promised her bear a photo shoot. Another promised to take her bear perfume shopping because "she is so worth it".
- One of the bears, Collette had a "weight issue" and it was a constant battle. As I parcelled her up I added a note saying she will be starving and losing a few pound by the time she arrives in the States and I got a message saying there will be a nice meal awaiting her when she arrives.
- Roberta, who is an over-size model has been sent to someone in the UK who told me "she has taken over the master bedroom

because she is large and in charge!" When I told him to get her a good quality mattress and good food he told me not to worry and that "she is having lobster Mac 'n' Cheese".

- Menopausal Iris was sent to a lady who says she could identify with her, yet she informed me that she thinks Iris is a secret gin drinker!
- Another lady in America assured me that Tracy will have her permanent residence near the Downton Abbey box set so she never forgets her roots!
- Henry arrived in the States and had to go straight to be to recover from his long flight!
- Edwina was excited to move into a new house with her new owner and her fiancé.
- And then there are the very touching stories with people often identifying with the little bear stories:
- A young lady shared with me that she has suffered anxiety and panic attacks all through her life and when I mentioned that I am writing the book she felt it is very relevant to a lot of people.
- The lady who bought dieting Collette, told me she also had weight issues and will tackle them together with her.
- A young woman going to university wanted to give her three adopted sisters a bear each as they all struggle with change and people leaving them. She wanted to soften the blow for these young ladies. I melted!
- Teddy Frank broke up with his long standing girlfriend as he had to move to his new owner in the States. He realised long distance relationships will not work for him. The person buying him sent a message saying how apt it was to have him as he also just came out of a long term relationship.

In short, I want to take people out of their reality for a short while and forget they are adults who have forgotten how to play. And play they do! And that makes me a very happy lady indeed!

Foreword

When Figen said she was going to write a book about her experiences with teddy bears, I had no doubt that within a few short months I would hold a crisp new published copy in my hands. Anyone who knows Figen will testify to her resourcefulness, her tenacity and her drive.

But teddy bears? Bears with 'issues', bears who struggle with OCD, health anxiety, bereavement issues and ones who can't get a grip on their wine consumption? How did they come into existence and how did their stories come to be told?

The answer lies in Figen's background as a therapist. For years she has not only listened to the whole gamut of human emotions and helped countless people with their problems, she has repeatedly pointed out the value of self-care and creativity. In the last couple of years Figen has had reason to take seriously her own advice due to health issues. And what began as a simple craft project morphed into a huge venture-she would say 'adventure'- linking her with people all over the world.

I was involved as a friend and have watched, sometimes quizzically, as teddy bears not intended as children's playthings, were knitted in various colours, photographed against a variety of props and had their brief back stories sketched out by way of introduction to their new owners.

The fascinating part was how the teddy bears became the medium through which the stuff of human existence was communicated. Those who had bought bears sometimes gave moving explanations about why they had been ordered. Then there was the humour that frequently surfaced as people in different parts of the globe pledged, in the spirit of Paddington Bear's luggage label, to look after their bear on arrival. Some of their comments are included in the book.

As the bears' popularity increased, the idea that a larger audience might be helped in a therapeutic way encouraged Figen to write more detailed stories which feature in the book. We also catch up with the characters after some time has elapsed to see what has helped them to resolve or handle their situations.

In all the years I have known Figen, she has been passionate about improving mental health and passing on information, techniques and skills to help others to feel better through her work as a counsellor, life coach, tutor and supervisor. She called her online shop 'Imperfect Hearts' to highlight the imperfections and individuality of people; we are human and share similar trials and triumphs. This book gives an optimistic message of hope that there are things, and people, that can help.

It is a mark of her generosity that Figen has donated significant sums from the sale of her teddies to local charities supporting mental health. Part of the proceeds from this book will be used to support counselling organisations.

Joanna Saatchi

My Journey

My name is Figen Murray, I am married with five children and several grandchildren. At the time of writing this I am 56 years old. I am a counsellor, counselling supervisor and life coach.

Writing this book has been one of the weirdest things I have ever done. I did not plan to write it. The thought just came to me one morning very early this year. The book was written within six weeks and I thoroughly enjoyed the entire process. I would often wake up with the next story in mind, waiting for an opportune moment in the day to eagerly type it up. My family and friends initially thought I lost my senses, however, as I went further along the journey the smiles stopped and were replaced by curiosity.

I guess I should begin by telling you the journey that led me going from an ordinary therapist to a mini-entrepreneur and eventually the author of this book. I've toyed with the idea of writing a book in the past, but never really knew how to approach it. I didn't want to write another counselling textbook – there are hundreds of those, and I was under no pretense that my knowledge was sufficient enough – but an unexpected turn of events led to me writing this book looking at life from the perspective of 16 knitted teddy bears. Life is a beautiful thing, but it can also prove complex and troubling at times. We all have our issues, and the next crisis or life event is often just around the corner. By writing this book, I hope to help people tackle some of those issues in a slightly more light-hearted way.

My story begins one morning when I had just stepped out of the shower. I noticed the sensation of trapped water in my ear. I shrugged it off, and aside from tipping my head occasionally to try and release it, I carried on with my day as normal. After several days, the sensation was still there, and I assumed I had caught a cold. That weekend, I went for a meal with friends, and my husband, who is a doctor, pointed out that I had struggled to hear a lot of the conversation. He had a brief look and told me everything seemed in order, but recommended a visit to my own doctor. The following day I booked an emergency appointment at my surgery and I was seen by a nurse who unfortunately mistook my condition for congestion.

I have since been diagnosed with a rare condition (1 in 20,000) called Sudden Sensory Hearing Loss and was told that in order to save my hearing I should have received steroids within 48 hours of my symptoms starting. My condition was not diagnosed until almost a month later by which time I also developed poor balance, tinnitus and severe hearing loss in my left ear. Despite eventually starting a course of steroids and having a surgical steroid injection, there was sadly no improvement. I can only liken my tinnitus to a permanent dentist's drill in my head. I am now the proud owner of a hearing aid with a masker built in to combat some of the effects of the noise.

The whole experience had left me feeling incredibly low, and I was also struggling to sleep due to the tinnitus. On my GP's recommendation, I reluctantly began a course of antidepressants. As a therapist, I know only too well how beneficial exercise is for mental health, so I decided to take up running to help improve matters. My husband joined me, and we regularly ran three to four times a week. It was an exhilarating experience, and improved my mental health vastly, but unfortunately my newfound happiness was to be short-lived.

I began developing aches and pains after running, and after seeking medical advice, followed by an x-ray, I was told I had the beginnings of osteoarthritis in both hips. The doctor advised me to stop running, and just like that, my moods began to plummet again. I had stopped taking on new clients as my hearing issue was making it difficult for me to listen and I found myself getting incredibly tired. With my mood at an all-time low, I decided to try a new approach.

I often encourage my clients to tap into their creative side, as creativity can bring calmness and balance in an often chaotic inner world. Taking my own advice, I purchased a range of floral fabrics and ribbon and began making vintage-style decorations in the shape of hearts. The psychological effects were amazing, and as I continued to craft, I felt as though I had mentally turned a corner. Before I knew it, I had created dozens and dozens of hearts, and eventually I moved on to more complex crafts, which is when I started knitting teddy bears.

My window seat in the dining room had almost taken on the identity of a craft fair, and upon seeing it, my daughter Louise suggested I started selling my crafts online, and introduced me to a shopping platform called Depop. She helped me list my items, and I decided upon the name 'Imperfect Hearts' for my store. My hearts represent the individuality and imperfections of human beings. As for the teddies my store motto is that as grown-ups we often forget how to play and the teddy bears are meant to bring a little of that playfulness back.

Unfortunately, my shop didn't receive any interest, and after months I had not sold a single item. A short while later, my friend Alison asked if I wanted to share a stall with her at a Christmas Fair, so I jumped at the chance and packed up my items. It was another failed venture, with people smiling and looking at my side of the stall, but not making any purchases. As the day went on, I found myself a little disheartened, and I text my son Martyn, explaining how frustrating it was that so much love, time and effort had gone into my crafts, only for them to be ignored, sending him a photo of the beautiful stall.

My son tweeted a photograph of my store explaining how heartbroken he was that nobody had bought anything, and in response, a few of his followers bought items from my online shop. I was incredibly excited that I'd made my first ever sale, and text him to thank him. After he tweeted my response, the tweets unexpectedly went viral, and I was inundated with purchases and requests for bespoke crafts. Before I knew it, the story had caught the interest of the worldwide media, and we were featured everywhere from the MailOnline to Buzzfeed to Good Morning America!

My Depop shop became incredibly active and I had to enlist the help of my daughters to help me pack and ship the hundreds of items I was now creating. I was so humbled by the experience that I started writing personal notes to go with each item. When listing my teddies, I started giving each one a name and an imaginary backstory, and I photographed them in various settings. In response, my customers started sending me their own stories, and telling me of ways in which they could identify with the characters I had created.

I was told inspiring tales of everything from bereavement, to weight issues, to anxiety and depression. It felt somewhat rewarding to have such a personal connection with many of my customers, and in my notes, I would often invite people to let me know how their teddies were settling in.

It was at this point that I felt inspired to tell my story, and realised it was the perfect opportunity to write a book. Having already donated a proportion of my earnings to a local counselling charity, I decided to channel my remaining energy into help of a different kind – a storybook for adults with a difference. Each teddy would be given its own story and tackle a common issue faced by adults, with a look into how that issue can progress over time, and the theory behind dealing with it.

I am delighted that this book has come to fruition, and could not have imagined the journey that led me here.

The Teddies

Claudia
Stress at work

Hi I am Claudia. I am 42 years old, single (again!) and live alone. I work for a multi-national company and have been with them nearly thirteen years. Love my job and have recently been promoted to Senior Account Executive - at least that is one good thing that came out of last year!

What a year 2016 has been! I guess it ended well with this promotion but the rest of it was not so brilliant.

I am just sat here with my lovely glass of Rioja after having had a nice long shower that ended ridiculously abruptly when I tried to do a bit of self-care. I thought I treat myself to this nice smelling new shaving gel and ouch…. I cut myself quite badly. So that was the end of my shower. I won't even tell you the language that came out of my mouth! Absolute filth! So here I am now sat in my PJ's watching any old rubbish on TV. I'm not really listening to it.

At work, I overheard David and Si talking about cutbacks the company needs to make. They were chatting about a meeting with the HR manager to discuss possible people they can get rid of. I found it so hard to focus on work today and that meeting this afternoon went on and on! Can Senior Account Executives be made redundant? I was the last one to be appointed. Last one in first one out. Isn't that what people say?

I love my little house. I needed a change of scenery after the break-up and decided to finally get on the property ladder. I can just about afford it and I have put my stamp on it and made it really nice. Can you imagine if I lost my job now just when I am finally settled! I met my neighbours for the first time yesterday; they are really nice and in a weird kind of way, I slept better last night knowing they live next door to me. I find it reassuring hearing the clickety-clack of Sandra's shoes as she is chatting to her children as she goes about her chores. And I like hearing the children laughing and having fun. Yes, it is good to live next door to someone when you live alone for the first time ever! Everything inside is all my taste! Tom always had something to object to every time we bought furniture or ornaments. I hated going shopping with him. The colour of the kitchen towels was wrong, the kitchen bin should have been a bigger one, the toothpaste could have been mintier. Thinking back now I really don't know how I put up with his constant whingeing for so many years. So yes, I think I am better off without him!

I often wonder how long Miss Fancy Pants will last? Bet they are sat watching Dragon's Den together. He wouldn't dare! That was definitely just our thing... We used to have so much fun watching it... No, he really would not dare making it their thing, too... I bet they are sat holding hands.

To think we were finally talking about getting married and making plans for it. Then he leaves his phone in the kitchen and she sends him a saucy message with a picture of her in pink underwear! Boy, was he in for a surprise when he came back in the kitchen! I don't know what hit him first, his phone or the engagement ring and then I charged at him and lost the plot completely. I dare say I broke a few things: glasses, cups, the toaster. Whatever was around really! That day lasted forever and it ended when I finally shut the door behind him as he left with all his stuff. I cried myself to sleep that night, and the next night and the one after that. And then one day I stopped.

Deep in thought I twirled my wine glass around, been doing this a lot lately; pouring myself a glass of wine. It really seems to relax me! But lately, I have been progressing to the second glass. I really shouldn't, it makes my head fuzzy in the mornings. Not brilliant when you have to present a new product design to the management board! And they all look so flipping serious and insanely critical of every word that comes out of my mouth! I think the time has come to stop feeling so damn sorry for myself... Sandra (my best friend and would-be maid of honour) has just started dating someone through this internet dating site. Roger seems really nice and a decent guy. He is into meditation and mindfulness and all that and runs a class in town. She keeps asking me to go with her. I might just give it a try and send her a text to say I will go with her tomorrow to the mindfulness class she has just started. Sandra would be the last person I thought would be into that kind of stuff but she loves it and she actually seems a lot calmer lately. And while I am at it I wonder if I should join that dating site. Now where is my laptop?

Six months later… Claudia is enjoying her mindfulness classes and has decided to go on a one week retreat in May to do meditation and mindfulness. She is so much more relaxed and her anxiety has diminished considerably. She swears by starting the day with a ten minute meditation and this really sets her up for the day. She is still single but has had a promising third date with a dentist. The crisis at work is over and she still loves her job. She no longer drinks wine to keep her anxiety at bay but enjoys the odd glass with a nice meal.

And another thing… Stress has become very intertwined with modern living. A lot of us use the word "stress" as part of our normal vocabulary. Our world has become increasingly fast paced, often frantic, particularly since technology offers us 24-hour connectivity.

With the proliferation of social media platforms for creating and sharing information and connecting people, comes an increasing need to stay abreast of the latest gadgets and what is trending. When you think of Facebook, Instagram, Snapchat and so on, there can be pressure to keep up with people. And while we may find social media use enhances our lives, there can also be downsides, both socially and in terms of our mental health.

In addition, our children are increasingly feeling the pressure with SATS and exams galore. This pressure starts early on in life and we are raising a future generation of adults who do not know how to switch off. Not surprisingly, mindfulness, meditation and yoga have become trendy as people seek to find ways to take care of their physical and mental wellbeing.

Of these, mindfulness is a word on many people's lips as more and more of us seek to learn how to live in the moment.

Gill, a friend and colleague teaching Mindfulness explains:
"To be mindful is to fully connect with our experience just as it is right now. So often we live our lives on "auto-pilot" never fully experiencing life as it is. Instead, as we go about our day we lose ourselves in thoughts of the past, things we did wrong (which we can't change) or worries about a future that may never happen. In truth, all we can deal with is this moment right now. Mindfulness is a way of staying fully present in our lives savouring the joy as well as facing up to the challenges that come our way. If we see life as it really is, moment by

moment, we build a truer picture.

There are so many ways we can bring ourselves out of "autopilot" and into now. You just choose to focus on one thing at a time (the absolute opposite of multi-tasking). This could be focusing on your breathing, the sounds you hear, the things you see or a specific task such as knitting. You bring your full attention to the task and every time your mind wanders (which it will) you gently bring yourself back to your original focus. Over time your concentration and ability to stay present will improve. It's a way of pressing pause on the day. Giving you a few moments of stillness amidst the busyness of life."

It is my understanding that new research suggests that in addition to enhancing everyday life, regular use of mindfulness can positively change areas of the brain. As this is not a textbook and I am not an expert in neuroscience, I simply direct the reader who is interested in understanding more of the science to investigate further.

As for meditation, it is a state of awareness where the mind is alert, yet calm and quiet. Again, that can only be good for us in this turbulent world.

Yoga is a traditional discipline initially practised in ancient India that involves our physical, mental and spiritual states of being. It is practised widely in the Far Eastern world and plays an important role in Buddhism and Hinduism. Again, I would encourage anyone interested to investigate Yoga in more detail.

It is my personal opinion, one I widely share with my counselling and coaching clients as well as my supervisees, that the most important word in any culture, language, religion or setting is BALANCE.

Without balance our ability to function in a healthy way becomes diminished. Mindfulness, meditation and yoga all help restore some of that balance and we would be wise to incorporate these practices or something similar into our lives, ideally every day. In our stressful world of constant change the latest gadgets, progress, news, expectations, goals to be met and pressure from all directions it makes sense to look into any healthy means to help our minds to quieten and give our brains a much needed rest.

Stress has become very intertwined with modern living. A lot of us use the word "stress" as part of our normal vocabulary. Our world has become increasingly fast paced, often frantic, particularly since technology offers us 24-hour connectivity.

Collette
Issues around food

Hi, I am Collette and I am 54 years old. I have just been to get weighed at my local slimming club. I lost two pounds last week and the same, the week before but sadly, I have gained a pound this week. Whilst visiting the cinema last Tuesday, I admit I had some nuts and a glass of wine but at least I stayed away from the popcorn! Well, ok, I had a couple of handfuls, but only because Mike, my husband could not eat it all.

Friday evening is 'takeaway night' and I am just not prepared to cook an alternative, healthy option for just me - it's easier to join in instead and order along with the rest of the family. But I just have boiled rice instead of fried rice and just a corner of the Nan bread. On Saturday, we went to a 50th birthday party. They had a huge buffet and I swear to God, there was just nothing healthy for me to choose. Not a single carrot stick or lettuce leaf in sight - it really is so hard to maintain a healthy eating regime!

I look at the various members of our slimming club... 'Fat club' some people call it but they are just so wrong! There is Susie, who has been a target member for two years now, she inspires me, I think "One day that will be me!" Then there is Lilian who has lost seven stone and Pete, who doesn't even resemble the 'Pete' from three years ago, he looks amazing!

Come to think of it, I've always had this weight thing going on. My dad used to tell me that I would end up fat and round like my mother - how I dreaded that mental image of me as a roly-poly! Not that my mother was as bad as that but she could have done with losing a few pounds; rather like me today!

Middle-age spread they call it. But, I prefer to say it as it is and call it 'blatant overeating!' Yet even though I know exactly what to eat and what to avoid, there are times when I know I have had my day's quota but I can't seem to stop, and carry on chomping away at anything I can find in my cupboards. People often say they are 'comfort eating' or 'stress eating' and at that point, I would love to pretend I haven't heard, and quietly walk away. But then my mind catapults itself back a few years ago to painful memories of constant arguments with one of my children, when he was a teenager. Goodness, how we clashed! He knew just how to make me react and was as skilled in pushing buttons as a Morse coder on a warship! We would argue, he would storm upstairs and proceed to slam the door behind him, whilst I would slam the door on my way to the shops to get my much needed 'fix' of Mars Bar, before returning to sit at the kitchen table, coffee in one hand, chocolate bar in the other, whilst I tried to calm down... and so the pattern would continue.

Now don't get me wrong, I am not an advocate of using chocolate or food as a means of de-stressing, but I guess I am just trying to make sense of what I did back then. Over-indulging in food was a very unhelpful coping mechanism that only resulted in me feeling tremendous guilt and shame about what I put my body through, by what I put in it!

It is the start of a new year and I am going to try very hard, to 'try hard' - if you get my drift? No, please don't read that sentence again - you did read it correctly! I have decided to keep a food diary, I will get myself a walking buddy (yeah, right!) and walk regularly, and I shall plan our family meals and shop more carefully. I am going to stop buying chocolate spread "for the kids". It is not for them, it's for me! There, I've said it! I buy it for me and I dig in when I need a chocolate fix. How disgusting is that! As for that cheese I buy for Mike? He can't even eat it as he is lactose intolerant! Wait! Hang on - I think I've said too much! All these declarations are making me feel very uncomfortable!

Six months later... Collette heard of a lady who was keen on walking regularly but did not do it because she thought it too boring on her own. So she contacted the woman and offered to be her 'walk buddy.' They have been walking five days per week ever since - their pedometer showing 4 km each day! Collette has worked out a four-week menu plan which she can rotate, so her family does not eat the same food every week. She now only buys the food she needs and no longer buys chocolate spread. If she needs a chocolate fix she puts it in the food diary she fills in every week rather than deny herself. So far, she has lost 12 pounds in total and the 'roly poly' threat no longer exists.

And another thing... There is no denying that a lot of people in the

Western world are overweight simply because we eat more than we need. In addition, our lifestyles may mean we are too inactive and we do not burn off unnecessary bulk.

However, we don't always eat through hunger. We live in stressful times and when we are under pressure, anxious, angry, insecure, depressed, frustrated or dissatisfied with life, one answer for some of us is to overeat. Eating can give comfort, make us feel more satisfied and compensate for all that bad emotional stuff.

On the whole we know what we should and should not eat. So when we overindulge we can also experience feelings of guilt and shame. We overeat to cover those feelings and a vicious circle is created. So: we stress eat, comfort eat, eat out of boredom, eat because it is in front of us and sometimes because we were brought up to finish everything on the plate. We may overeat as a form of self-punishment and self-harm. There are no doubt other reasons too, as the supermarket shelves are groaning with tempting food and the advertising industry really pushes it. Interestingly, when we watch people indulging in adverts they are never overweight but are often a perfect picture of health.

Being overweight can bring with it feelings of low self-esteem as we can become self-conscious about our appearance. Going to the beach or a public function where society expects us to look "good" can become a nightmare, as nothing seems to fit or look ok. If the media's image of the correct or most desirable body shape doesn't tally with our own, we can feel a sense of failure that we don't match up.

As well as psychological issues, it is important to bear in mind that being overweight can lead to a range of severe health problems, such as stroke, heart disease, high blood pressure and diabetes. To maintain a healthy lifestyle it is important to have a well-balanced diet and exercise regularly. This does not necessarily mean spending hours in a gym. It can be as basic as going for a brisk walk regularly to get our hearts beating just that little bit faster or buying a step counter to try to walk the recommended 10,000 steps a day. Other plus points are having a good sleep routine and balancing work with relaxation and fun activities.

Of course there are certain eating disorders such as anorexia nervosa, bulimia, binge eating, compulsive overeating and other related disorders. These are conditions that often require in depth psychological help and specialist counselling, as well as hospital treatment in more severe cases.

We don't always eat through hunger. We live in stressful times and when we are under pressure, anxious, angry, insecure, depressed, frustrated or dissatisfied with life, one answer for some of us is to overeat.

Juliette & Ellie
Bereavement & loss

Hi I am Juliette and I am 39 years old. I have a 12-year-old daughter called Ellie. She and I are usually very close but recently, she is starting to get a little hormonal. She has begun to answer me back, admittedly only on a couple of occasions, but it's so out of character for her! Once or twice, when I have tried to initiate conversation with her, she has grunted rather than reply properly. I can feel it in my waters that this is going to be the start of many moments of teenage hell, with her dishing out her teenage Angst, and me trying to dodge the emotional punches that will no doubt come at me from all directions. That's going to be one hell of a few years! I seem to hear a lot of 'problem' stories from other parents about what a nightmare their child was when going through their 'teen years.' I do hope she is not going to freak out and act like one of them!

Lately I seem to have these worries and can't shift them. I am a single mum, all thanks to Tony, who didn't come home one day! Oh, please don't look so worried - I am ok with it all now, honestly! That was a long time ago - six years to be precise. He was a driver for Langton Bakery. He worked there ever since he left school. School was never his thing; he was just not academic at all. When he passed his driving test, they eventually offered him a job as one of their drivers. I guess it made a change from the production line and at least he had no more night shifts - although the down side was, he started at five am every morning! But that suited us perfectly, as he finished by two pm, in time to pick Ellie up from nursery and eventually school.

I was one of the receptionists. We flirted with each other once in a while. I really fancied him as he was quite a dish! We actually started dating right after our Christmas do. I'll never forget the date as it was December 2000 – Millennium year! Oh, it was blissful! I was 23 years old and finally had a proper boyfriend! Fireworks were going off in my heart, alongside the many thousands that littered the sky that night! I honestly thought my heart would burst with joy! We married a couple of years after that and I fell pregnant a year later. The three of us were so happy, I was proud of my little family and life was good!

Then came the knock on the door and a policeman and a police lady stood there. My knees buckled before they could even speak. They did not need to explain why they were there - I knew what they were going to say! So yes, we had a few difficult years, Ellie and I. The funeral, the tears, lots of people around us, and then, eventually, they disappeared one by one. We had lots of support from family and friends that first year. They helped us through the first Christmas without him, followed by Father's Day, Ellie's birthday and the many other significant days without him. Then they seemed to disappear, and we had to face the second year and all the important dates and many milestones that would follow, alone and without him. Somehow people seem to think the second year is no problem. I don't blame them! Before this, I would have thought the same but as death has touched us, I now know it takes much longer than the first year to cope with these important days. Ellie and I spent many nights crying ourselves to sleep in my big bed that I used to share with her dad. United in our grief, we would hold on to each other, both lost and confused for what seemed an eternity. It took me over two years to shift his pyjamas - I simply could not bring myself to get rid of them! Writing it down, it sounds ridiculous to admit that I needed to smell his scent on them in order to fall asleep – I did wash them eventually but not for a long time.

The school were so supportive towards Ellie. They organised some counselling for her and someone worked with her for about eighteen months afterwards. Slowly and gradually, she became the happy little girl I knew before it all went so horribly wrong - whilst I became a 'widow'. Such a horrible cold and unfriendly word! It conjures up all sorts of images in my mind's eye, in particular, a dark-cladded spinster with hairy warts. Not unlike Nanny McPhee before her magical transformation to the lovely Emma Thompson. Now I am definitely not in her league - that's for sure. I am a little on the small side and an average size 12 to 14. In addition, I have red hair and freckles - unfortunately, nothing like Emma Thompson! But looks aside, I guess a lot of men and women become widowed at any age, sadly. That's life!

I decided to start some bereavement counselling myself, and saw this lady for about eight months. That was so helpful, not just with coming to terms with losing Tony but with so many other things. I needed to access my future and what to do with it. Counselling helped me look beyond my pain and actually helped to ease it. I will always miss Tony, but I also know that life carries on, and Ellie and I need to carry on.

So Ellie is poorly with chicken pox, at the age of 12 that is quite unusual I guess, as she never had it as a little one. Her young cousin picked it up from nursery a couple of weeks ago and as we were at his fourth birthday party soon after, I guess that is how she got it. She looks a little flushed and is rather hot and bothered but definitely still okay to demand we play 'Jenga' and cards. Ellie is amazing at card games and I bet her dad is watching over her, whispering some 'cheats' into her ear. If he was here now, I know the two of them would wink at each other (their signal) to get the better of me!

My food shopping order has just been delivered, all healthy and all vegetarian. Ellie and I made the decision to become vegetarian on New Year's Day. I wonder how long it will last and who will cave in first? We are both suckers for chicken stir-fry and that is usually what Friday night consists of: stir-fry and a movie.

I am so glad I ordered my usual bunch of roses. That is one thing I have continued to do since Tony died. Without fail, he would buy them for me every week. Don't get me wrong, I am not in the least extravagant but he knew that to make my home a place I felt happy in, I always had to have a small bunch of roses on my kitchen table. It always puts a smile on my face and I spend many a moment looking at the roses, whilst thinking of Tony. Not in a sad way – but more in a 'fond memory' kind of way.

I never intended to tell you this story in so much detail and certainly did not wish it to sound sad. I hope I have not depressed you. That was not my intention. Please don't worry as I am really very happy - life is what it is and I am making the most of it. I'm just sat watching Ellie, who is having a little feverish snooze. We make a good little team together, her and I.

I should really finish my essay whilst she is sleeping - only the conclusion left to do and I already know what I am going to say, it's just a matter of typing it up. Oh, I totally forgot to mention - a few years ago I began studying again and I am just in my last year of a media degree. One more essay and finally my dissertation to do. Then that's it - I will get my life back!

Six months later... Juliette finished her degree and got a 2.1. She has a second interview with a small advertising company, ten miles from her home. One of her friends has organised a blind date for her which she is both dreading and looking forward to in equal measures. She has not even thought about being in a relationship since Tony died but she did not dismiss her friend's suggestion, when she mentioned it to her. Ellie is helping her find an outfit for the night out. Her moodiness has increased but she still describes her mum as her "bestest" friend!

And another thing... Death is often such a dreaded word for many of us. Yet we rejoice when a new life arrives in the shape of a baby looking up at us. Beginnings and endings are part of the cycle of life. However, for a number of us death is devastating and the impact is enormous, often life-changing.

Different theories around death talk about various stages of grief. Sadly, grieving is not as straightforward as some of the theories might lead us to believe. When our world is shattered by a loved one's death, whether it was expected or sudden, we fall apart. It can feel like a journey of zigzag. One moment we can feel despair, the next we can feel hope only to go through despair again when we least expect it. We experience sadness, anger, shock, disbelief, guilt and so on. We can feel the sheer horror of having to go on without them, the physical pain of loss, and often feel totally lost ourselves. There is no linear way of grieving as it is such an individual thing and it is a journey every person has to travel in their own way.

When someone we love dearly suddenly dies it is inevitably a massive shock and it is likely that at some stage our minds will turn to "if onlys" and "I wish I had said or done this or that". An example happened in my extended family recently following the death of my uncle who developed HAP (hospital acquired pneumonia). Despite the fact that before he was admitted he had been in very poor health and according to the doctors was slowly dying, his loving daughter felt wracked with guilt because she had agreed to his request to be taken to hospital. However had she not taken him and he had died at home she would never have forgiven herself either. So feelings of guilt can be an enormous issue.

Losing people we love is one of the most painful experiences of our lives and there is no shortcut for our feelings. We need to go through emotions of extreme shock, sadness and devastation. Sometimes people can feel anger towards the person who has passed away. They feel abandoned. In some cases there may be anger directed at medical professionals, the hospital or someone else. Anger is a normal feeling to experience in bereavement and often we look to blame others rather than acknowledge how we feel.

The emotional rollercoaster and nightmare will diminish at some point and bring us gradually to a place of acceptance. But how long this will take is very individual. We hear of people remarrying after a year of losing their life partner, and then there are people who struggle with their bereavement for many years. There is no set time frame for this journey of emotions.

Supporting a bereaved person through their first big anniversaries (birthdays, Christmas, wedding anniversaries, Mother's Day, Father's Day and all other important dates) is a kind thing to do, however it is important to be aware that support is often needed and appreciated in the second, third or subsequent years. People often feel abandoned after the first big anniversaries are over. A text message, card or a short phone call may be all that is needed for a person to know they are not forgotten.

Claude
Porn addiction

Hi I am Claude. I am 37 years old and am from the Burgundy region of France. To be more precise, I come from the historic region of Beaune, and about twelve years ago, whilst helping out in my parent's business, I became actively involved in many autumn wine sales. (I come from a long line of wine merchants and approximately three decades ago, my parents took over the family business.) Anyway, whilst I was working there, I met my wife Susan. She is from Stoke-on-Trent in Staffordshire, UK. Susan, along with a couple of friends, was on a working holiday at a nearby vineyard and when I met her one evening in a local bar, it was definitely love at first sight.

We have been married almost ten years and have two wonderful children. Sophie, who is five years old and Lucien, who is three. Susan runs her own hair salon, two streets away, whilst I work from home. I am a freelance journalist and write for English, American and French newspapers, as well as some financial and political magazines. We have Adeline, our French au-pair looking after our children. We chose a French au-pair so she speaks to our children in French only as we desperately want them to be bilingual.

So I am off to the attic room for most of the day, locking myself away to work for hours on end. Without wishing to blow my own trumpet, I produce really good work! I have plenty of articles to write and a solid list of regular clients who throw work my way. But I have to be honest with you – it's not only work that takes up my time when I am in my little room. In fact, some days I am unable to focus much on work! You see, about two years ago, I discovered internet porn and what a world it has opened up! I thought I knew everything there is to know about sex but over the past few months, my laptop has opened my eyes to things I did not know were possible! I never intended to start all this. I mean, I always guessed most men look at porn and I bet a lot of women do! But how I started, it was all quite innocent. Wasn't it?

It happened when Matt, Susan's brother was staying with us. He initially came to stay for the night, when he was going through a rough patch with his wife but ended up staying about six weeks! He left his laptop at work one day and asked me if he could use my office upstairs to finish a report before going to bed, and I of course agreed. So you can imagine my surprise when I switched my laptop on the next morning and realised he had been looking at lots of porn sites. My first reaction was bewilderment, closely followed by outrage and embarrassment. Anyway, I promptly deleted it all and carried on working but the whole day left me really unsettled. So, later on, I hit on the Search Engine 'History' tab and decided to have just a little peek at some of the stuff whilst I was having my lunchtime soup and sandwich. Well, I can tell you that it was not just my soup that was steaming hot that day! That evening, I felt really awkward around Susan and the kids and what's worse is the fact that I sneaked back up there after tea to "finish off an article". Needless to say there was no article to finish! But during my brief half hour up there, what I did see, got me awfully excited! I frantically clicked on more and more images. Wow! I couldn't believe how it made me feel! That night I had the most amazing sex with Susan!

To be perfectly honest, I don't even know why I do it. Initially, it was just harmless fun, something that blokes do! But it slowly occurred to me that accessing porn helped me with my feelings of guilt concerning my parents. I am an only child, their business is up for sale and they desperately wanted it to stay in the family and hoped that I would take it on. Don't get me wrong, I absolutely love wine and can tell you everything there is to know about the industry - which wine will complement a particular meat and which matures well and tastes better with age. But other than drink the stuff and enjoy it with a fantastic meal, shared with good friends, I have no desire to work with it and besides that, I have never wanted to work in the family business. My father and I have always clashed and it just wouldn't have worked. So the guilt is eating me up inside and when I look at all that 'stuff' online, it takes it all away, transports me to a different world, a world where I am totally guilt-free.

Thank God I pay all the bills and they are all in my name. Susan is very respectful of my privacy and would never dream of opening my mail. What a shock she would have if she saw some of the bills! You see, the problem is that over the past year I have progressed to live action porn. I subscribe to people who perform privately, just for me and as it is in real time, I can ask them to do anything I want them to do - and I mean, anything! I have to confess I am a regular customer and they charge by the minute and I'm talking £2.00 per minute! Hefty bill this month, I mean really hefty, I've just received a £394 bill! This cannot continue, it is madness! I finally plucked up the courage to confide in a mate of mine the other day and he told me of a friend of his who had the same liking for porn. This guy was given an ultimatum by his wife to sort himself out or get out! He was found out after his daughter went to upload some family photos onto his laptop from her phone and found pornographic material on it. That could easily have been me! I shuddered at the thought. My friend thought it best I talk to him. So we met. His name is Mark and he told me of this group he goes to every week. He is doing something called a '12 step programme.' How am I supposed to do that? To attend every week when I never go anywhere! What will Susan think I am doing? I don't want to lie to her, yet it feels like I have been lying to her for the past two years, so I have to come clean. This is weighing far too heavy on my mind...

"Susan? Shall we go out for dinner tonight? There is something I need to talk to you about?"

Six months later... After a lot of distress and a near decision to end her marriage, Susan decided to support Claude with his treatment to combat his sex addiction. They now both talk a lot more. She had no idea how he felt regarding his parents' business as Claude always kept his cards close to his chest, but that is different now. They spend regular time together and talk about things openly.

Claude also no longer works in the attic and instead, has taken over the snug as his new office. He leaves the door open as he has nothing to hide. Anyone going past can see he is actually working and not looking at inappropriate material. Claude has joined a sex addiction group, where he works on overcoming his addiction. He has also engaged in 'one to one counselling' with a specially trained counsellor.

Claude flew over to France and had a frank and honest conversation with his parents about how he felt. His parents told him not to worry as they felt that there is a lot of competition from much bigger merchants these days and they had been running the business at a loss for the past twelve months. They went on to say that they are looking forward to having the money from the sale of the business and plan to go on cruises and travel the world in order to enjoy their retirement years.

And another thing... Porn addiction is when a man or woman is overly preoccupied with pornographic material, these days mainly on-line. People need no longer ask for questionable magazines from under the counter or smuggle very liberal videos from abroad. Everything is easily accessible by pressing just a few buttons in the privacy of our home. The porn industry is a fast and ever increasing multi million pound industry.

Porn addiction can cause problems amongst couples as the other person may often liken it to infidelity of their partner. When porn has become an addiction it may become more difficult for a person to function in loving relationships, the person may develop sexual dysfunction and may start distancing themselves from their partner, family and friends. The person may isolate themselves not only to access material but also due to feelings of guilt and shame.

A person addicted to porn may start neglecting other activities such as looking after their health in terms of diet, exercise, sleep or self-care in general as they may feel compelled to access material to an increasingly obsessive level. As with most addictions the need to "use" more often and with porn addiction more explicit material is a constant issue to achieve the same level of satisfaction. What may have disgusted the person at one point in the past now appears unexciting.

This addiction may result in some people spending vast amounts of money to pay for costly live action sites or to visit prostitutes on a regular basis. The latter may lead to health risks such as sexually transmitted diseases. Sometimes people can risk getting into trouble by accessing material at unsuitable places (such as a work setting or someone else's laptop).

Help is available by means of support groups and twelve step programmes where people are assigned a sponsor who guides them through the steps. The sponsor as well as the group provide an important support network and ongoing help, particularly when temptation beckons.

Using any electronic devices in a more public place within the family such as the lounge or dining room rather than a bedroom or an office at home offers more transparency and trust amongst family members. Allowing family members access to your search history also helps reassure others around you and contributes to re-establishing a more honest connection with either your partner or other family members. At this point it is important to state that one big step in the right direction is to redefine sex, love and intimacy altogether. These are three different things entirely. We can have intimacy by just the way we share our togetherness as people, be that to just look at each other lovingly or just have a kiss and a cuddle without having to have intercourse. Intimacy is just a deep seated closeness and understanding between two people. Love is how two people feel about each other. It means a close emotional bond and deep fondness. Sex is a physical act between two people and can be executed without love and intimacy.

When people recover from porn addiction it is essential to form healthy attachments with people based on respect, true affection, trust, love and intimacy. Sex should not be top of the agenda without these other factors.

It can happen that all these feelings can sometimes get confusing and therefore a solid network of support will help enormously on this journey.

Yvonne
Vicarious trauma

Hi my name is Yvonne and I am 46 years old. I have been a therapist for 22 years now and I love working with people. My head is full of hundreds of people's stories and my job is really rewarding. Connecting with people on such a deep level is a total privilege and I am absolutely certain that a lot of the things people have told me, have never been told to another soul and never will be. So, I am a keeper of secrets- many of them!

What's that? You want to know some juicy secrets? Not a chance! I am not allowed to tell you anything. My lips are sealed - my work with my clients is confidential and I am bound by my Code of Ethics.

What sort of situations do people bring to me? ... Ah, well, that is something I can tell you. People come to me with depression, anxiety, self-esteem issues, relationship issues, uncertainties about their sexuality or sometimes porn addiction (that is about as juicy as it gets!) They may have problems at work, decisions they are finding hard to make, OCD behaviour, bereavement, addiction, stress, completely awful work/life balance, social shyness, problems with blushing, general unhappiness (without knowing why), abuse issues of any kind. The list goes on.

And before you ask, yes, I can sleep at night! My training has taught me how not to let client material affect me. That is so essential, I tell you! And yes, occasionally a client will totally get under my skin. But hey, I am only human! I also have to have supervision - that helps a lot, too. But I know what you mean. One could easily think that counsellors' heads would explode with all these stories - I used to think that too!

Providing therapy is not the easiest job I have ever done. Before I retrained, I was a PA to chief executives in various sectors in industry. Giving therapy is quite a bit different to managing your boss's diary or arranging board meetings with full agendas in place. But it's had its juicy moments, like the day my boss asked me to ring the company's regular florist to send his wife an anniversary bouquet. Of course, it was also deemed my responsibility to remind him of their anniversary! Anyway, no sooner had I put the phone down to the lady, I heard my boss's other door open, then a female voice. The muffled conversation turning into a heated argument, then a door being slammed. Moments later, my boss stormed into my office with a furious expression on his face. He asked me to order another bouquet for our personnel manager (a single mum, half his age with two daughters). I asked him what message he would like on the accompanying card... "I am sorry. It won't happen again!" came the answer. So, 'Happy anniversary,' Elsa – of course, I will never divulge what he just asked me to do! I will keep this secret, along with the secret about his bottom drawer at work being full of chocolate bars (no doubt supplied by the lovely personnel manager! That was taking people management a little bit too far!) So you see? As I said, I am the keeper of secrets.

Oh, I do side track, don't I! Anyway, getting back to therapy. As a therapist we see the pain, feel the despair, sense the insecurities and anxieties, and if truth be known, it can zap our energy. So we need to be fairly rested on a mental level and fully available. No easy task when we have life going on also! Therapists have their fair share of crap happening in their life, too and I cannot even begin to tell you how irritating it is, when people say to me "You are okay, you are a therapist, you can cope with that!" So what are you saying? I cannot be affected by anything as I am, 'sorted?' Ah... No! I do not spend half an hour a day in front of the mirror doing therapy on myself. Would be good if I could though!

So when we are with our clients we need to be entirely focused on that person, listening to every word, noticing every twitch, hearing any fine nuances in their speech, taking on board every eye movement or tapping of feet or fingers, listening out for repetitions of key words, hesitations, intakes of breath, etc. You are listening with your ears and eyes and you also have to be aware of what is going on inside you whilst you are with the client. So many aspects to consider! So yes, it is quite intense work. But it is a pretty cool job!

I should undergo therapy from time to time. That is also written in my Code of Ethics. Self-care has to be really good in order to stay well-balanced, when you do this kind of job. But I guess that I should not be arrogant enough to think mine is the only job that totally zaps your energy! I am thinking of people like ambulance drivers, people in the police force or fire service, people who work as Samaritans, soldiers or grave diggers who have to lower tiny white caskets into the ground whilst watching parents dissolve in their grief. There are so many jobs that are difficult, in terms of what people see, hear, witness and what they give of themselves. For example, a priest who often has close family connections and hears a lot of painful stories, youth workers, people working in prisons, social workers, people in the army, doctors, nurses...The list goes on. I never really used to think about these things until I became a therapist. I remember someone once telling me that a train driver, on average, witnesses one suicide around every ten years on the tracks. How absolutely awful must it feel, hurtling towards a human being at high speed, knowing full well that the brakes are not going to stop the train on time! The driver would be completely traumatised! What about firemen finding people burnt to death or prison staff walking into a cell and seeing someone hanging there? These kind of terrible tragedies will of course, cause considerable trauma to them! So there are many jobs out there where we get damaged in small instalments – the technical term for it is: vicarious trauma. Yes, you heard right! It is recognized as trauma. Every trauma we hear, see or witness leaves a little bit of the trauma behind, and little by little it accumulates.

I have yet again closed my list to new clients as I have a lot going on at home. You know.... family stuff, health issues. So I need to slow right down and let people go on a waiting list. That is fairly easy for me as I am a private practitioner, but other employed people out there, may not have that luxury. So be aware! Take the time to find out, before you begin working for people, whether you think you could cope in times of need.

Six months later... Yvonne has had five months weekly, personal therapy and it has given her a chance to offload some of the difficult things going on in her own life. She has let go of some things she has no control over. She has also decided to take her advert off a therapist directory and will decide in six months if she wants to open her list up again this year or take a break for a while. Thankfully, she is not totally dependent on the income. She has contacted every potential client on her waiting list and referred them to other therapists, explaining to them that they will not be able to see her in the near future due to health reasons. She has also firmed up her boundaries and decided to see her clients within a set three days rather than spread them out over five days. This gives her a better work/life balance* which she puts to good use.

*Also in The Code of Ethics, mentioned earlier in the story.

And another thing... We all know people who have had bad things happen to them. We have bad things happen to us. As humans we experience loss, bereavement, rejection, illness, physical and emotional abuse, divorce and arguments, anger and threats. We may deal with immense pressure at work and sometimes at home. And most of us get on with life and try to take these things in our stride. We build resilience and inner strength.

It is not to say that people like therapists, soldiers, fire fighters, police officers, social workers, doctors, nurses and many other professionals who work with people are not resilient and cannot cope with seeing and/or hearing awful stuff. But when this exposure is constant we bring some of the grief, pain, hurt, distress, anger, confusion and despair into our own lives. The technical term is Vicarious Trauma, also known as Compassion Fatigue or Secondary Trauma.

It is my strong belief that people who hear traumatic stories or who see traumatic events on a regular, and sometimes daily basis are damaged in small instalments. Sadly, what we hear and see as workers in these professions can slowly and silently inform our view of the world. The bit of damage that is left behind has an accumulative effect that can negatively affect our emotional and physical wellbeing unless we exercise high levels of self-care.

As a counsellor the need for self-care is incorporated into my professional body's Ethical Framework that informs my practice.

Helen, a fellow counsellor who teaches on the subject of vicarious trauma, says it is crucial for us to be aware of some of the warning signs: feeling irritable or angry at the slightest thing, personal relationships suddenly feeling more difficult, headaches or migraines creeping in more and more, feeling forgetful, feeling tired or not sleeping as well and maybe drinking a little more alcohol than usual after a long day at work. We may also feel a greater than normal level of responsibility regarding our work and may find it harder and harder to want to do the job we normally love and enjoy.

So how exactly does self-care work? Our Ethical Framework states that therapists should engage in activities other than counselling. That can be difficult when looking after the needs of others comes more easily to us than looking after ourselves. A good work/life balance is crucial and giving ourselves permission to invest time in things we love doing is not an indulgence but a necessity. This will be different for everybody as some people unwind by running, gardening, decorating, abseiling or taking part in other very active pastimes, while others enjoy doing a jigsaw, knitting, painting, singing in a choir or reading romantic novels.

Another side of self-care is eating a healthy well-balanced diet, meeting up with friends and family, treating ourselves to a favourite latte, having a pamper session or simply having time alone doing nothing much at all.

Ensuring regular breaks, not taking on too many clients and having holidays are also important. Doctors, soldiers, fire fighters and those in other professions mentioned earlier will no doubt need to find similar ways to ensure they look after themselves.

Helen says it is not possible to stop vicarious traumatization from happening as it is the price of caring. However we can always try to reduce its impact with effective self-care.

Lucy
Hoarding

Hi I am Lucy and I am 39 years old. I am married and we have two girls. They are twins and are approaching their 17th birthday. They are great girls and I just love them to bits! But they can be hard work, as many teenagers are. Lately, they have been moaning about me storing various things in their bedrooms. It is not much really, just a couple of bin liners in each bedroom. One of them is full of pink Christmas decorations – this year, I decided upon purple and white, so for now, the pink is redundant. The other bags are full of their old baby clothes – so in theory, they should not moan about this as it is their stuff! One day, when they have their own children, I'm sure they will thank me for keeping it all.

The other day I asked why none of their friends come round anymore. It wasn't so long ago that the house always seemed to be full of noisy, excited girls enjoying regular weekend sleepovers. In a way, it's a pity as they both have massive rooms and the house really lends itself to having lots of people visiting. Although, I have to confess, that these days, I am not so keen to have visitors. It's awkward as people have to climb over my stuff - I have a few things in the corridor by the front door, you see. Just a few boxes, some old magazines and newspapers that will come in handy, besides, some of them I have not even read yet. Thinking about it, there is not actually much room on the sofa either for people to sit. I'm looking forward to starting my knitting, I have bought some beautiful wool and am also waiting for some to be delivered from eBay – a fantastic bargain, a job lot of fifty balls for next to nothing!

I really should do some washing, but there is still some on the line that needs to be taken in and folded. Shame that I can't quite access the back door at the moment – I bought a new kitchen bin on Monday and I am not quite sure where to put it yet. I will find a place for it. So at the moment I'm unable to move around much in my kitchen. It will all get sorted! I promise!

Not quite sure why my husband keeps telling me to throw stuff away. We have so many arguments! He wants to throw away the picture frames that I found in a skip the other day. You would not believe what people just throw away! I found some perfectly good suitcases, frames, a chair - okay the wood has split on the seat but that can be fixed. I just can't bear people wasting stuff! So I bring it home with a view to repair it or put it to good use in some way.

Family life can be strange, can't it! My husband sits in the armchair by the television, and watches it continuously, even when there's nothing interesting to watch! We rarely speak and we don't eat together as a family either. The girls disappear with their food in one of the bedrooms and watch TV, Eric sits in his armchair and eats his dinner, watching sports, whilst I usually eat in the corner of the dining room, on the window seat. The table has some stuff on that I will sort out soon and I plan to go through it all. I know I will definitely tidy up soon, but I just don't seem to have the time. The girls aren't really helping and Eric never has, so I just stopped tidying and cleaning. After all, if they don't care why should I?

Eric and I had a row again about money - he says I spend too much. But I just buy what we need, well, most of the time anyway. Someone was selling a job lot of toiletries the other day, a real mixture of stuff. I couldn't pass up on a bargain like that, so I bought it all - £180 worth! Ok, the girls don't like any of the stuff and Eric does not use anything other than the shower gel but there are about 300 toilet rolls amongst that and everyone needs toilet rolls! Right? I would give some to my sister, but I will not let her come into the house anymore. The last time she came was about 18 months ago and she said that my house smells and is too jumbled. I have no idea what she meant. I think she was just looking for a reason not to visit!

The girls have been asking to go to her house to get ready for Prom night. She only lives two streets away, so why on earth they want to do that is beyond me! The house used to be so full of laughter and chatter from the girls' bedrooms, with their friends constantly coming and going. They used to bake together, dance in their bedrooms and generally acted really silly, the way teenage girls do, and I miss all that banter they had with their friends. I would chat to them and enjoy their friends being here but I guess the girls are probably a bit embarrassed about some things. The toilet is not very clean, you see. I would clean it but there are just so many things piled up in front of the sink that I'm unable to access the cleaning materials underneath. Besides, it will get dirty again anyway.

So this is me. I live my life, feeling enriched with all these objects and things around me and I love being surrounded by it all - it makes me feel happy and secure and all warm inside. The things that have accumulated on the dining table are mainly old newspapers, but I have to read them, it would be a waste not to! If anyone ever asked me about current affairs, I definitely want to be able to answer them, but how could I do that without reading the papers? I know a lot of people use the internet but I prefer to have something in my hand to read, it seems to make more sense that way!

And the two filing cabinets I bought will definitely come in handy. When I get round to it, I will be able to sort through all the papers on the settee which will enable Eric to sit in his favourite place again. Looking at the pile of papers, I'm at a loss how to file it all. There is an assortment of bills, insurance documents, school correspondence, car tax forms and pension information, so I obviously can't throw it out, I just need to figure out what goes where and categorise it and I also need to find a place for the filing cabinets, they are bigger than I thought they would be!

It isn't that I don't want to tidy it all up, it's just so damn difficult to know where to start. Last week I was so determined to clear things out and then as I looked around, I panicked - I literally did not know where to start. Instead, I ordered a pizza for us all. It was far more enjoyable and allowed me to avoid thinking about how I should have been tidying up. The other day, I came home with some cheap baby stuff: baby blankets, a baby alarm, cot sheets, bottles and teats, scratch mittens. I was thinking that when the girls have their children I will have acquired quite a lot of baby clothes and accessories for them. Oh, look! That pale green baby grow would have looked so good on Josie! Such a shame the girls never got to know their older sister - she would have been nineteen this month!

Six months later... Lucy got rather upset and spoke to the twins about their forthcoming Prom. She said she would get champagne if they got ready and left from their home instead of their auntie's house. The girls sat down with Lucy and told her how embarrassed they were about the state of their house. Both girls felt too awkward to invite any friends round and had been feeling that way for quite some time. Up until that moment, Lucy did not realise that she had a problem - she had been in denial for a long time.

She spoke to her sister and finally allowed her to come to her home. Her sister stayed calm and suggested she would find a therapist to help Lucy overcome her hoarding issue - Lucy had not even realised that what she was doing had a name! During therapy, she realised she had not grieved properly over Josie, as she was pregnant with the twins when Josie died of cot death. Lucy is on the mend and a specialist therapist comes to the house and helps her dispose of some items each week, gently talking her through things. The house is beginning to get back to a normal state and the girls have started to invite their friends round again. There is a long way to go yet but Lucy is progressing.

And another thing... Hoarding has finally been accepted in recent years as a mental health issue. It is often triggered by trauma, particularly bereavement or loss. People can also be genetically pre-disposed to hoarding tendencies.

Hoarding is when a person's living space becomes very restricted or almost impossible to move around in, due to the gathering and accumulation of items that are often not needed, or even useless to the person. The prospect of throwing things out can cause them great distress and severe anxiety.

They may want to have a tidier space but feel totally overwhelmed about making decisions about where to start and what to keep, worrying that items may be useful at a later point or that they may run out of things. If others attempt to help tidy up, it can cause a lot of stress as the hoarder may be upset at people touching their stuff.

Often people begin to isolate themselves as they become more and more embarrassed about letting others into their home. When hoarding happens in a family setting, everyone can experience increasing difficulty living in a place that is so cluttered. It may be impossible to cook family meals, as the kitchen surfaces are crowded. Children no longer have a safe place to play as danger lurks around every pile of items, gradually suffocating a once tidy home.

The house becomes potentially unsafe and possibly even a fire hazard as genuine escape routes may be blocked by piles of stuff. Family members can also become isolated, as they feel too ashamed and embarrassed to invite people round. Sometimes people get into financial difficulties due to an almost compulsive need to buy more and more items.

Help is available, although this is often a lengthy process. Hoarding can be treated with Cognitive Behavioural Therapy, as this will help the person change the way they feel about amassing items and it is hoped that this in turn helps change the way they think.

Goals can be set as part of this very gradual step-by-step programme, with the hoarder staying in control of the process throughout. Often family therapy is necessary for the hoarder to recognise the impact on others, and to establish how the family can help the person progress. Therapy will also deal with triggers that may have started the hoarding behaviour in the first place.

George
Seasonal affective disorder

Hi I am George and I am 38 years old. I live in Manchester, UK, and guess what Manchester is really famous for... Yes, rain! You know the stuff that comes pouring down on us far too regularly!

My family and I live in a lovely, big Victorian house with a beautiful garden. I am a house husband and feel really uplifted in being one - a couple of my mates also have the same job. Thankfully, we now live in a day and age where it is more accepted, and so it should be!

I had the patio redone a couple of years ago to enhance our outdoor living experience! (please don't laugh!) We bought a sizeable table and chairs for outside - it really looks the part. One moment, there's a draft coming from somewhere. I just can't deal with being cold. My fingers are all stiff as I write this. Anyway, back to the table... It was meant to be for entertaining the family, having barbeques outside, enjoying a late evening, whilst enjoying a cool bottle of beer. But for the past four months, it has sat in a sheltered part of the garden, covered up, to protect it from the elements! It gets me so down! I look outside at this oversized monstrosity and think "what a complete waste of money!" It honestly makes me wonder why people in England bother buying garden furniture. Who are they kidding? Al -fresco dining in the North of England? Yeah, who am I trying to convince! Furthermore, manufacturers insult us by selling patio heaters. Have you ever lit one on the first half-decent day we get after winter? Goodness me! Scores of spiders crawl out from everywhere! Have you ever been in the path of panic-stricken spiders? I shudder just thinking about it!

Every morning, I feel tired and my body aches. I am finding it so hard to get out of bed, in fact it is tempting to jump back in instead of straightening it every day. Then I lie there, psyching myself up to quickly jump in the shower and defrost!

It's time I booked a holiday. Problem is, my wife is really hard to pin down. She has a very important job, you see! One week just to go somewhere to bask in the sun's rays would be great. Oh yes! A quick family holiday during half term, over to one of the Greek islands, or maybe Turkey, or Cyprus perhaps? You know, I would even be happy with a week in Benidorm! Honestly!

Actually, right now, to have any extra daylight would be amazing. It is 8am and still dark! All the lights are on in the house, and scraping the ice from the car window, I find myself wondering if my tongue would stick to the windscreen, if I licked it. Weird thought, I know. But hey, that's me!

Today is the first day this week that I haven't had a patch on my back! You look puzzled? Here, let me explain...Last Sunday, whilst decorating, my back just went! You know, in that scary way where you're literally unable to move for some time! And no, I definitely was not doing the Mannequin challenge! I was rooted to the spot, unable to move and terrified to try and attempt to! Has this ever happened to you? "Hexenschuss" they call it in German, roughly translated, it means "witch's shot". Rather like (I imagine) being struck by a witches' wand! Anyway, I was unable to move for some time. Luckily, after what seemed an eternity, it eased off but I was plagued all week with lower back pain. But as they say, every cloud has a silver lining, and for me that was, drum roll please...heat patches. Wow! I just love them, particularly in the winter! Not only does it take the edge away from the pain but......oh my goodness, it blissfully and steadily warms my back for a whole eight hours! Reading this through, I sound as if I am addicted to the patches? No, honestly, I am not, but I have to admit, thanks to the heat patches, I felt less cold this week. However, no patch today and I just cannot get warm. Wouldn't it be a great idea to produce them for people who struggle with the cold. If they can offer hand warmers, then why not have 'all over' heat patches' for an entire back. That's the place where I feel the cold the most! I would buy in bulk; I swear to God!

Every morning when I go for my walk (a brisk one I might add!) it depresses me that every person I meet seems dressed for an Arctic expedition! With their hunched disposition, they are almost bent-double, in a bid to escape the unforgiving wind that insists on blowing its icy cold breath at them. Seriously, I just want to book this holiday now! I honestly need to disappear.

Did I tell you I am a regular at the doctors every winter? Flu jab! Antibiotics for chest infection, gel for my aching joints. Then there are the anti-depressants...Yes, I take them every year during the winter months. I feel so down, fed up and miserable. Why is it that everything just feels so bleak and dismal this time of year? The doctor told me I have 'SAD,' which is short for Seasonal Affective Disorder. He went on to say that there are thousands of others like me! Can you believe it? I honestly thought it was just me being a really miserable beggar every autumn. To explain it more simply, It is as if someone flicks a switch at some point around October and Bang! There you have it, I'm struck down with SAD and the real me does not appear again until the clocks change back in the Spring.

Did something sneaky today – I stuck a travel brochure in my wife's bag! Not very subtle I know but I really think the time has come for us to book a holiday. I know that will cheer me up immensely. Believe you me, the whole family would benefit from me cheering up! Not that I would openly admit it to them but I am so grouchy during the winter months.

Oh this is just the best part of the day sitting near my SAD lamp. It's doctor's orders, so I'm only following them! It's my daily treat! Cup of tea in hand, I close my eyes and just think about shimmering blue oceans, golden sandy beaches, the scorching sun and...Oh for the love of God, would someone please shut that door!

Six months later... I am full of energy these days! We have just celebrated our 15th wedding anniversary, and my wife and I decided to disappear for a few days. So we booked one of those uber-cheap bargain trips to Sorrento. It was only four days but the weather was glorious! Obviously not quite warm enough to make use of their outdoor swimming pool but the hotel was boasting spectacular views over the town and the sea. The sea there is crystal clear and we really enjoyed our long chats walking along the endless beaches, it was just what we needed! Now the children are getting older, their grandparents quite like them staying over for a few nights, so we need to do this more often.

Upon return, I feel completely recharged and somehow, in a much better frame of mind - and the best is yet to come. We booked a family holiday last week in July. Two weeks in Cape Verde. Sun, sea, a couple of books to read, music downloaded ready to go and getting in the holiday mood this weekend. We are off to the shops to buy a few bits for the holidays!

When we finally had some space to chat over a glass of Vino in Sorrento we decided that we have finally reached a stage with the children where it is okay to leave them for the odd long weekend with the in-laws or my parents. And there are plenty of amazing offers for a quick escape to the sun. So this will be a regular thing in the future! Already have a four-day trip booked for September: a city trip to Istanbul. Yay! Can't wait!

And another thing... SAD is in simple terms a winter depression, that kicks in when the nights get longer, the temperatures drop and the seasons change to the winter months.(Sometimes it happens the other way around where people get SAD in the summer months, however this is much more rare.) The symptoms are similar to depression: e.g. feeling hopeless or worthless, having anxiety, not wanting to get out of bed, waking up early or having sleep disruption, aches and pains, changes in appetite often resulting in overeating carbohydrates, a complete lack of energy and having difficulty concentrating.

There are varying degrees of SAD. The most common is Sub-syndromal SAD which is a bit like having the winter blues. This is when people generally just feel lower than they would in the summer. According to SADA (The Seasonal Affective Disorder Association) (www.sada.org.uk) about 21% of the UK population have Sub-syndromal SAD while a further 8% suffer from full blown SAD in such a way that it makes day to day living quite challenging and often medication or talking therapies are used.

Sub-syndromal SAD brings with it lethargy, the need to sleep more and eat carbs but it does not bring depression and anxiety to the extent that the person can't cope.

If you find yourself suffering from SAD rather than Sub-syndromal SAD it may be worth seeing your doctor for some medication and a possible referral to some talking therapies. You could also invest in a light therapy lamp which has proved quite helpful for some people. Spending as much time as possible (using sun protection creams) out in the daylight, particularly on sunny days will be of benefit. But it may also be worth considering taking a holiday somewhere sunny during the winter months rather than spending all your holiday allowance and finances on a summer holiday in August.

The symptoms are similar to depression: e.g. feeling hopeless or worthless, having anxiety, not wanting to get out of bed, waking up early or having sleep disruption, aches and pains, changes in appetite often resulting in overeating carbohydrates, a complete lack of energy and having difficulty concentrating.

Martha
Exam stress

Hi I am Martha. Yes, it is an unusual name. My parents gave my sister and I, slightly old fashioned names: my sister's name is Elsie. I actually rather like my name. There are about 1,500 kids in our school and I think there are only two of us with the name Martha. The other one is in one of the lower forms. On the other hand, there are thirteen Megan's, five Emilia's, 7 Charlotte's and 9 Olivia's. The boys are just the same. With an assortment of Alex's, Oliver's and Sam's. Our year group has around 160 people so you can see why I like my name, it is distinguished, classy even! Ha!

If you have not yet gathered; I love numbers. I also love Maths. In fact, my mum has just given me an envelope with a confirmation slip and a cheque, which will enable me to enter an additional further Maths GCSE exam. Maths, for me is easy – I just get it and I am forever explaining mathematical equations to my mates when they don't understand. I don't mind really; I like to help them.

Christmas holidays this year were a bit of a flop as I could not really enjoy myself properly. We had mock exams as soon as we came back in January. January 5th, to be precise. And guess what? That is my birthday! Yeah, happy 16th Martha! Oh, and by the way, let us start today with not one, not two but three exams! Yes, they actually made us sit three exams on day one of a new term! Can you believe it! We had eleven exams in total, spread over two weeks. The last exam was just about tolerable as Mr Peterson was one of the invigilators. Little does he know that literally all the girls have a major crush on him! It was fun having him walk up and down during the exam and quite a welcome distraction.

So my birthday this year came and went without any real celebrations. It was definitely overshadowed by all the exam revision I did. We had Biology in the morning and English Literature immediately after lunch. Everyone was so irritable, all we talked about was 'The Secret River' and 'The Merchant of Venice.' Emily, my best friend, was really stressed out about the Shakespearean one, as she said she had not revised it well. We were arguing about what the possible questions could be.

I am one of the lucky ones as I am quite good in a lot of subjects, although my favourite is still maths. I get mainly A*'s and maybe the odd A grade. Some of my best friends struggle here and there and we all help each other out when we don't understand a subject. But to be honest, I am also a little apprehensive about getting my results. Don't get me wrong, I can't wait for them, because I want to do really well. I want to have straight A*'s - I am very competitive. My dad says I am just like he used to be at school. Thanks Dad! But it is really hard to be very openly happy about my results, as I know that some of my friends will get terrible grades, and the last thing I want is make them angry or maybe feel that they are in some way, beneath me.

This year is our GCSE year, so the marks really matter and will determine our future! Although the mocks are over now and we have our results (yes, I did really well, all A*'s apart from one A) everyone is just that little bit more miserable. It feels like the calm before the storm. We all have this gloomy feeling inside as everyone is acutely aware of time running out until our actual exams start in May and June.

The German exchange students arrived on Thursday. Jonas is staying with my friend Harry and they live just down the road from me. Jonas is so fit! Harry called me to say that we should all go for a pizza, followed by the cinema. Jonas wants to see if he understands a whole film in English! Please God, let him sit next to me... And... he is. Thank you, God! I owe you!

Easter holidays at last! We are off to Lanzarote for a week and my parents have made me bring my revision notes. Not sure why really, as there is an abundance of material on the internet. All I need is my iPad and Wi-Fi, but try telling that to my parents! Adults are definitely complete dinosaurs, when it comes to technology these days! School gave us some brilliant websites and a list of YouTube mini lectures to watch. Elsie even times me when I do the revision papers in the hotel room while she is busy putting her make up on to go out for dinner later. I just take ten minutes to sort myself out. I am not into make-up and all that yet. Although, I hope that cute waiter is serving us again downstairs. Maybe a little bit of make-up is okay. Makes me look at least one year older than I am!

So the holidays are over, everyone is stressed out, and I mean everyone! The teachers are unbearable now! Some shout at us, the others cram our heads with stuff. Guess they are under pressure, too! We tried a get together last weekend, six of us! They all came to mine as my house is the biggest and we have a sleepover room downstairs in the basement. We were all so emotional! ...Nope, you are wrong. We were not on a period! None of us were. It was just pure unadulterated outpour of exam emotion and we were all on the verge of a nervous breakdown. So we finished watching "The Devil Inside" and three of us went across to the shops and bought two carrier bags full of sugar..... Well, sort of. What we bought was strawberry laces, Haribo's, jammy dodgers, Party Rings, Donut and ice cream. Ben & Jerry's obviously! Need you ask?

So we pretty much gulped down all that sugar and were finally on some sort of sugar cloud and temporarily were sort of normal. You know?! Giggling, chatting, gossiping, prank calling Will who we all fancy! And then came the inevitable sugar crash. And with the crash came the tears. We had a communal cry. Everyone knows exactly what I mean. You can't go through teenage years these days without a good communal cry! But eventually we all fell asleep.

Four months later... My photo is in the school newsletter alongside quite a few of my friends. We had our results and of course I managed to get straight A*'s all the way through. I could not wait to send a message on my family WhatsApp group, really trying hard not to constantly grin about my results. I hugged one or two of my friends who did not do so well and cried honest tears with them as I genuinely felt for them. We only went in first thing at 10 am to collect our results. I looked around the room and Sam jumped up and down waving his papers in the air. He did well, I guess. Henry was quietly sat smiling gently. He did well, too, I guess! Some people were hugging and either laughing with tears of joy or crying and comforting each other as they were upset. So much emotion in one room!! My friends and I wandered down to Pizza Hut. Lisa's mascara was quite smudged from all the crying she did. We all took it in turn to sit with her and hug her and make her laugh....I just love my friends!

And another thing... Exams, tests and interviews are all part of our busy lives. Most senior pupils are used to being tested on a regular basis throughout the school year, yet the GCSE and A level exam periods are a particularly stressful time for many students. The number of different subjects that pupils need to revise for at GCSE level brings additional demands.

Schools give guidance about study timetables and study skills. They do many revision sessions and some hold study clinics during lunchtimes or immediately after school on a drop-in basis.

During this season, students can often struggle to fall asleep or have disrupted sleep because of exam worry. Some suffer from headaches or migraines while others have constant backache. Heightened anxiety can affect concentration at precisely the time it is most needed. The inability to concentrate in turn increases anxiety even further and students are often trapped in this cycle, becoming more agitated and irritable. Appetite is another area that can be affected.

It is really important to build in regular breaks, some form of sports activity, and a healthy diet in particular breakfast, fresh fruit and vegetables. Young people need a good eight hours sleep and should stop revising at least a couple of hours before bedtime, doing something completely different in order to unwind and relax.

Talking things through with their peers who understand the pressure they are under helps them to see that they are not alone in their stress and also students can encourage each other, both in terms of the revision they have to do and in taking a break.

Listening to calm music and doing something creative will also help. In contrast, what does not help is excessive caffeine in its various forms, including energy drinks and energy pills, which can all disrupt and disturb sleep.

A further piece of advice to students: don't compare yourself with your mates. Attend as many extra revision classes as are on offer for the subjects you find hard. Exams are such a big and important part of our educational and professional life but there is life after exams. Honestly!!

A further piece of advice to students: don't compare yourself with your mates. Attend as many extra revision classes as are on offer for the subjects you find hard. Exams are such a big and important part of our educational and professional life but there is life after exams.

Jennifer
Obsessive-compulsive disorder

Hi, my name is Jennifer and I am 44 years old. I am a manager at a large college in the town. There are in excess of 30,000 students a year and about 600 of them pass through our department. I actually never intended to end up in management, I really wanted to teach therapy. I actually am a therapist; I also work privately from my home. Anyway, one day I just had this strong urge to pass my knowledge on, and I ended up here, teaching the topic to small groups of students. I used to pop in to the college with my teaching material, go straight to the classroom, and feed the students' minds with something a little different than their regular subjects. Teaching talking therapies is not like teaching history. Ask any therapy student!

Then, every once in a while, I would go to the office to see my boss, just to touch base and check he was happy with what I was doing. It was a large open plan office and he usually sat in the corner with three other people. There were thirteen people sharing the office altogether. I hated going in there, as there was stuff everywhere: stacks of paper and folders, phones would ring, the photocopier would hum, doors would slam and people would talk loudly. Not surprising that I always left his office feeling rather frazzled!

So, get this, he comes up to my colleague and I one day and tells us he is taking early retirement and would the two of us be interested in applying as a job share. Now, I have to say, that was something I had never even considered! We went home that day and thought about it as we promised we would. The following week Hannah approached me and said she would like to job share and I felt the same, so we applied. The interview brief was a ten-minute PowerPoint presentation, so I prepared my part. However, on the day of the interview, Hannah dropped a bombshell and told me that she had decided not to go for the job. So I was interviewed on my own and that's how I got the job.

First day in my new role, heart pounding as I sat at my new permanent desk. It was set out in a way that there were four desks in a block, i.e. two desks mirrored by two opposite desks. Frankie and Louise, who sat opposite me, were both social work teachers, whilst Lewis, next to me, was doing teacher training. It was a busy setup but we were three departments sharing one office.

As I looked around my desk and allocated shelving, I noticed that all my folders were really ancient and frayed at the sides plus the paper inside was not very neat. The backs of the folders had different styles of handwriting on, with various words crossed out, Tipp-ex had been used on them several times and some of the locking mechanisms were not working. I stopped, suddenly aware of a loud thumping noise...What on earth was it? I looked around and everyone was working. It took me a moment or two to realise it was my heart pounding! My hands were beginning to sweat and I could feel a sensation as though my throat was beginning to close in, I began to gulp several times, it seemed as though I was running out of air! There was I, surrounded by chaos and people and I realised I was about to have a panic attack. I quickly picked up my car keys and handbag and told Lewis, that I would be back in half an hour.

Away from the office and with a definite goal in mind, I slowly began to calm down and I could hear my heart rate returning to normal. Slowly, slowly, I took long deep deliberate breaths, the panic had gone and I felt relief...now where was the office supply shop?

Yes!! Bin liners, twenty lever arch folders, but which colour? Hmm...purple? Yes, a good calming colour. Ten box files in the same matching colour plus a matching pen holder and three stackable trays – also matching! I arrived back in the office, feeling in control and better equipped to begin my new job. The department secretary and I spent the next couple of days changing all the folders and files over to the new box files and she typed me lovely neat labels that all LOOKED THE SAME! Thank heavens! Finally, some sort of order! Initially, people laughed at me but then one or two of them eventually muttered that they should follow my lead and have a good clear out.

My first year as a manager plus my first year of teaching a major course and I found myself inheriting hand-outs from previous lecturers that were photocopied dozens of times. Some not legible, some not even photocopied straight. Mental note to myself 'need to sort this!'. Painstakingly, I typed up every hand-out neatly! Arghh! That damn phone is ringing again! I attempted to busy myself with my paperwork whilst my three colleagues all beckoned to me to answer.

Don't look! Don't listen! Do you not realise how awkward I find it talking to people on the phone, when there are lots of people around me? Realising I could not evade it, I tentatively picked it up "Jennifer speaking, can I help? Pardon? Oh, (louder) Jennifer speaking, can I help?" Cringe! Thank God, one of the other phones was ringing. Louise was now talking to someone, and yes! Lewis just got up to photocopy something. That made the phone call so much easier. I found situations like that extremely stressful and difficult to cope with.

Every night, upon arriving home from work, the first thing I do is put the kettle on. Goodness! Who on earth put the mugs in the cupboard like that? They shouldn't be stacked! And why are the handles not all pointing to the left? Luckily, the cleaning lady has been that day, so at least I don't need to worry about cleaning...Just nipping to the loo, arrgh! She has done it again! The soap always goes to the right of the tap, whilst the hand lotion is on the left. And why have the kids not taken the empty toilet roll downstairs?! Here I go again, I need to wash my hands twice before I leave the bathroom. Isn't it logical? Once to wash the dirt off, once to wash them clean! Obviously!

It is finally Saturday! No work, what a glorious feeling! I get myself porridge for breakfast and find the empty box left in the cupboard, again! And actually, why on earth are the boxes so messed up? I had aligned them all, and very neatly might I add! There, that's better! Alison and Paul have popped over for lunch, so I bustle around and add the finishing touches to the home-made soup. We have some lovely fresh, crusty bread to accompany it and houmous, olives, and a side salad. They are all sat around the kitchen island, watching me open the cupboard and Paul suddenly bursts out laughing! What's so funny? I raise my eyebrows and question him. My spices? In alphabetical order? Yes? Of course? Aren't yours? Doesn't everybody do that? Immediately, I blush with embarrassment. I don't know why I place them in alphabetical order. I always like to put order into things, but that's just me. So, ok, I have a touch of OCD! I embrace it as it helps me have a little bit of control in a chaotic world.

His reaction did make me think though. I guess I assumed that everyone is like me. I always thought I am just super organised. But actually, I just prepare for eventualities and I just try to have a little control when a situation totally freaks me out. The episode at work, and when I took the job is such a prime example. You see, what I omitted to tell you earlier, was that at the time of me taking on the job, I did not think I would need to work near several people in an open plan office, and I certainly never thought that I may need to speak loudly on the phone with so many people listening. I was terrified of being judged for what I said on the phone with all eyes on me. I also did not know how to send emails, let alone send attachments and was completely out of my comfort zone. Embarrassingly, the secretary had to discreetly show me how to do this, during one lunch time. I also had no idea how to write a monthly management report, which was required of me. So all in all, I was highly stressed and my work life was so out of control, so teaching the odd class was a welcome respite.

The first six months in that job were absolute hell. Every morning, I would make the journey to work, feeling nauseous and sick with worry. In my distress, I felt compelled to park in the same spot each day, and if the space was taken, I would feel very unsettled for most of the day. I had to wash my hands several times a day, particularly when I knew I had to make a phone call that everyone was able to hear - it would take a couple of toilet trips and up to seven or eight hand washes, to build myself up to it. My journey home in the car was guided by numbers that determined how the next working day would be. If my tachometer ended in triple figures or certain patterns of figures it would be ok. To elaborate; the following numbers were ok: 34534, 34343, 35000, 35035, 35555, 35656 and so on. It had to be certain patterns and I had to witness the switch over to those numbers whilst driving. Stressful and dangerous when you have to watch the traffic but so significant and reassuring to know it would mean I cope better with tomorrow. I would be lost without my OCD, but lately I have relied a lot on these numbers. Don't get me wrong, I don't work at the college anymore, in fact I stopped teaching altogether and just work from home these days. I shouted at my daughter the other day for not paying attention to the tachometer. We both share my car and while she was out driving, the tachometer reached 37888. I was so annoyed with her, she knows how important that is to me! Ok, I just read that back and realised how ridiculous it sounded!

Six months later... Jennifer has covered the mileage part of her tachometer with masking tape so she is no longer distracted by the numbers. She could have of course, gone to therapy to sort this issue out for good. But there are two things she considered: firstly, she is a therapist herself and understands why she has always resorted to these behaviours in times of stress, and she is looking for other ways she can try to cope with stressful situations. Secondly, some of her OCD behaviours are okay for her to keep. She now defends her spice cupboard as a sensible way of storing them alphabetically. When she makes curries she uses up to 11 different spices and it is so much easier when it is all sorted that way. No rummaging in her cupboard, there is nothing wrong with that!

Jennifer now pays more attention when her anxiety levels are up, at this point, she will grab her walking shoes and go for a half hour walk to reflect and also clear her head.

And another thing... OCD stands for Obsessive Compulsive Disorder and as the name suggests sufferers often have reoccurring obsessive thoughts or urges that can be distressing and are almost impossible to shake off.

Obviously, most people check that their back door is locked or the iron is unplugged, but with OCD this often turns into an increasingly time consuming and pressurised ritual. The person may check the back door not just once, but establish a routine where various things have to be checked several times and they are unable to rest until this extended task has been accomplished.

People who suffer with OCD can sometimes engage in excess cleaning routines involving their environment or themselves because of a fear of germs and contamination. There may be a cleaning compulsion to wipe surfaces and areas again and again, or to carry out repeated hand washing.

Sometimes the sufferer seeks reassurance through numbers, or order, or some form of symmetry. Their world will be okay for example, if all the labels in the cupboard face forward, or they have walked up the stairs three times. A lot of time may be devoted to unnecessary rituals like sorting and resorting cupboards and other areas. Sometimes there is a fear that if certain routines are not carried out, something bad will happen to themselves or others. The time these tasks take can gradually increase and the pressure can mount.

Obsessive thoughts can be disturbing and upsetting and may for example be of a violent, sexual or religious nature. There can be fear at the idea of losing control, or doing something terrible to themselves or others.

Talking therapies can be of enormous help in challenging obsessive thoughts and rituals and people can learn how to change dysfunctional thinking patterns such as catastrophizing (e.g. "If I don't put all the books on the bookshelf in size order, something will happen to my partner.")

Cognitive Behaviour Therapy is one of the most commonly used approaches for the treatment of irrational beliefs and thoughts, which many people have found effective.

The Cognitive Behaviour Therapy treatment may have an 'exposure and response' element to it where, for instance, someone with a fear of germs in public places may be encouraged to handle things like door handles, loose coins or something touched regularly by others. The person is then encouraged to sit with the anxiety for as long as possible. It is anticipated that the strong urge will gradually diminish and over the period of treatment, the need to wash hands may be reduced to a healthier level.

Talking therapies can be of enormous help in challenging obsessive thoughts and rituals and people can learn how to change dysfunctional thinking patterns such as catastrophizing

Malcolm
Relationship issues

Hi, I am Malcolm and I am 59 years old. Wow! That feels so old when I say it out loud! I shall be sixty in two months and my wife, Saskia is asking me what we should do to celebrate. She wants us to go on a big trip to Dubai. Ha! It's her dream to see that city, but not mine! She likes the urban architecture, whereas I just see it as a dusty city built somewhere in an Arab state. So, definitely no desire to go there! But unfortunately, what she says, usually goes. Without a doubt, she definitely wears the pants in this house!

Being this close to sixty has made me re-evaluate my life and think about my future, our future to be precise. Saskia is 62 and closer to retirement than I am, but to be fair I am thinking about how many more years I should work. I am a solicitor and love my job. I really enjoy working with my clients, and feel so energised when I am able to help someone with a major dispute or a complex divorce. I also adore my colleagues. Since we started the practice, about thirty years ago, Pete and I have been the senior partners, then there is Rachel, who handles conveyancing and Monica who deals with probates. We try to offer a wide range of services. We took on Abby recently who is our expert on family law. And then there is Becky... Rebecca Morton to be precise. She is one hell of a legal secretary and has been with us for approximately fifteen years, since she first started as an apprentice.

One day, we were working on a big case and we needed to get things ready for court, the case was rather tricky and we worked until very late. Well, one thing led to another and we have been secretly seeing each other for the past six years. During this time, we have had a few hairy moments. As she is divorced, we mostly go back to her place when her kids are out at their dad's. But obviously, when her children are around, we have to resort to using the office, it's not ideal but we don't have many choices. Anyway, my office has a very comfy sofa, goodness, if that sofa could talk, the stories it could tell! Once Pete came back to pick up a file he needed for court the following morning, needless to say, there were red faces all round! Another time, the cleaner decided to come in the evening instead of first thing in the morning. I just about managed to zip up my trousers before she breezed into my office, duster in hand! Luckily, Becky had turned to face the window to button up her pink blouse! I love that blouse! It always turns me on! I can see her bra through it and the material is so silky!

So going back to retirement, it's going to be difficult as Saskia and I don't really have much to offer each other anymore. We have been married thirty-three years, straight after we finished university. Well, we kind of had to as she was six months pregnant and both sets of parents insisted we tie the knot. So we did! Don't get me wrong, initially, our marriage was great. First Bobbie was born, then Danielle. Of course, they are both grown-ups now. Saskia was a great mum, still is! She looked after all of us really well, but somehow we drifted apart. I was busy building my practice and making money for the never-ending demands of the family. Saskia also insisted that both children went to private school and I don't need to tell you how expensive that was! So, while I was busy working, Saskia was busy spending money, oh and meeting friends for endless lunches and coffees! As well as going to the gym and generally filling her time with non-essential stuff. As the kids got older, sex at home stopped. The standard reply I always got whenever I asked was "We can't, the children might hear us!" I mean, who in their right mind has to book into a hotel in order to have sex with his wife. By the way, that only happened every couple of months when we could persuade one of either set of parents to come and babysit. Sadly, somehow, over the years, I fell out of love with her. If I am honest, we drifted apart and somewhere around this time, she became very secretive and began hiding her phone or disappearing outside when it rang. Looking back now, I think she may have had a brief fling with someone and I'm ashamed to admit it didn't bother me. Who am I to talk anyway!

Becky is so much fun and is up for sex any time! In fact, she will occasionally tease me at work and brush herself up against me in the kitchen, when I'm sorting out my lunch and nobody is near. She is also extremely intelligent and we have really interesting conversations. It makes me painfully aware that at home, all Saskia and I talk about is the children (even though they have both moved out now.) Failing that, we do general small talk about the neighbours, the news, current affairs or who won at tennis! No more holding hands, no cuddling up to each other, no more sex! The last time we had sex was almost seven years ago, just over a year before I embarked on my affair with Becky! The sex life I had with my wife just seemed to dwindle away to nothing, until one day it was non-existent. You know, I can't even remember when she asked me if I minded having twin beds? I must have agreed on one of those occasions when I was not really listening properly. I remember feeling really taken aback when I went to bed one evening and there staring at me, as if they were mocking me, were twin beds! For my part in it, when did I stop really listening and most importantly, when did we stop caring?

The only time I really think about Saskia and I is when I sort out my antique china collection in my office at home. You see, I occasionally like to have a decent cup of tea, Earl Grey is my favourite. So I sit in my office, with my feet up on the window sill. It has beautiful views over our garden and is so peaceful and tranquil there. As I drink my tea, I often find myself staring intently at the porcelain china cup I am holding and it takes me right back to when we first met. There was this antique shop near my student house and I would often go there and buy the odd ornament or plate - that's all I could afford then! Piece by piece, I would take it home to mum and dad's every time I visited home. That's where I met Saskia, in the antique shop. She was studying English Literature and Philosophy and had taken on a part time job in the shop.

As I reminisce, this overwhelming feeling of sadness comes over me. I remember fondly that I often compared her to one of the delicate and dainty items I used to buy from her. She was a treasured thing that became very precious to me. What on earth happened? I could cry a million tears as I fail to understand just how we fell apart and became like two distant strangers. I may be turning sixty soon but I'm not old, I wonder if we should maybe talk to someone?

Six months later... Piers, who I regularly play squash with, mentioned in passing that he decided to go for relationship counselling as he was going through a difficult patch in his marriage and he said it really helped redefine his relationship with his wife. I plucked up the courage and told him about Saskia and I and he listened patiently. He then got his wallet out and gave me a business card of the person who they went to see.

Whilst having my Earl Grey the following weekend in my little study I thought long and hard about what I actually want from my future and this is when I decided to speak to Saskia. Interspersed with many tears she admitted that she was very unhappy in our marriage and she was desperately wishing those old times when we were still a proper couple were back. She also told me she knew about Rebecca Morton as a colleague of mine was married to the brother of one of her friends. She told me that the affair was common knowledge at my law firm. I was mortified to hear that!

I arranged to meet Rebecca the following morning and told her that I had decided to make another go of things with Saskia and that we should no longer continue with what we were doing. We tried to work alongside each other for several weeks but it really did not work out. She was getting upset, I was constantly tempted but my mind was nevertheless made up to mend my marriage with Saskia. Hardly surprisingly, Rebecca handed in her notice a couple of months after I finished with her and I must admit it was a huge relief!

Saskia and I started relationship counselling and after initially spending quite a lot of time arguing and crying in the sessions we have now progressed to finding new ways of interacting with and relating to each other. We have started – wait for this – ballroom dancing lessons and we both enjoy it tremendously! This is giving us a whole new range of friends. Also, we have demoted our twin beds to the children's bedrooms as they had both turned into storage and junk rooms after they moved out. We now have a beautiful king size bed with a built in television at the bottom. So we enjoy late night movies whilst cuddling up to each other in bed. And yes, sex is back on the menu! Sort of.....work in progress....Get my drift?

And another thing... We fall in love, we get engaged and then get married, we have a few children and we suddenly stop playing as things get a bit more serious. Children need a lot of focus and attention and parents have to work harder to look after and finance the ever increasing demands of the growing family. A lot of the day to day conversations centre around the needs of the family, the children, their friends, their school. In all that busyness of family life we often forget to take care of the relationship, the very thing that made the family thing possible.

People can drift apart though for many other reasons too, not just a busy family life where parents are often inevitably pulled into different directions.

Sometimes it happens that for no apparent reason people grow apart, develop different interests or goals and their world view suddenly does not match up anymore. Some couples fail to nurture their relationships by downing tools as relationships are in constant need of looking after – by both people.

Relationship counselling can help a couple learn better ways to communicate and how to listen to each other with respect and kindness. It can also help a couple identify where it all went wrong in the first place in a constructive rather than destructive way.

Of course there is no relationship without a crisis and relationship counsellors can show a couple how to handle arguments in a better and safer way. The couple can also learn how to express and own difficult emotions. Any changes that may need to happen for the relationship to continue successfully can be negotiated in the safety of the counselling room.

Obviously, not all relationships can be saved in this manner but counselling can also help people to part amicably and respectfully, which is even more important if children are involved.

Oliver
Coming out

Hi, I am Oliver and I am 29 years old. I am gay, confident and have a great circle of friends. I'm the only one of my five thousand siblings who is single, so my friends tend to take the place of my boyfriend at family parties. It helps that I have an amazing family, and my friends love both my mum and stepdad and my dad and step mum. When I think of some of my friends whose parents have never accepted their son's or daughter's sexuality, it makes me realise how lucky I am.

It hasn't always been this cushy though; coming out was a difficult experience. I built it up so many times, but always chickened out last minute and snuck back upstairs to listen to Mariah Carey. Looking back, that in itself probably gave the game away without me even needing to say anything! Anyway, I did eventually manage to tell my parents, although not in the way I had planned...

I was 16 and it was my long awaited high school prom. Me and five of my friends piled into our limousine and were chauffeured to the venue by a very strange man (we'd booked it on the cheap, lesson learnt!). He drove us around town with music blaring out, before finally arriving at the venue.

We had the most amazing night – a sit down meal followed by a disco. It was weird seeing our teachers out of the context of school, but some of them were pretty good dancers, and we had a great night with them! I seem to recall straying from my prom date, Harriet, in the hope that the attractive PE teacher, Mr Simons, would fall madly in love with me and whisk me away, but alas, it was not meant to be.

Some of my year group went into town after prom to celebrate the milestone, whilst others (including me) headed to house parties to celebrate with friends. When the party started to lose steam, I staggered home at 4am with Sally, a friend of mine who lived two streets away from our house. Sally was absolutely wasted, and I tried to walk her home, but she was throwing up and was terrified about getting in trouble with her parents. I brought her back to my house, took her up to my attic room and fed her water. She was such a pretty girl, what a good job she came home with me and not some of the other guys in my year.

"What is going on? What the hell are you doing? Oliver, wake up, now!"

My eyes opened and I saw the outline of my mum and stepdad! I had fallen asleep with Sally in my arms, with my suit jacket wrapped around her. Her short prom dress was hidden and her legs sticking out – it was obvious what they were thinking. Cue lecture from my stepdad about unprotected sex. I knew I had acted irresponsibly by bringing her home, but I thought I was doing the right thing in looking after her in the state she was in. Needless to say, when Sally left that day I was grounded for a fortnight! There was another party I wanted to go to the following week, and I couldn't bear the thought of staying in for two weeks in the summer holidays, so I decided the time was right to spill the beans.

I headed downstairs to speak to my mum, who was alone in the kitchen. "Mum, can I talk to you for a second? Can you sit down?" I said nervously. She replied frantically, "Oh god, Oliver, what's happened?" I tried to tell her, but nothing came out. "I'm too scared to tell you. You won't get it... I can't say it!" My heart was pounding and I felt sick inside.

Mum looked at me and smiled, knowingly. "You're going to tell me you're gay, aren't you?" I froze. "How did you know?" I exclaimed, "I'm your mum! It is my job to know!" she laughed. She came over and gave me a hug, and I cried tears of relief mixed with tension and fear of what was yet to come. What about the rest of my parents? What about my grandparents? My list of worries were endless. But it was time to tell the truth. No more feeling awkward when my gran asked me if I had a girlfriend yet, or squirming when my granddad moaned about the gay characters in Coronation Street in front of me.

My stepdad, stepsister and brother were all totally cool with it – again, all stating that they already knew. Looking back at home videos of me prancing around like a fairy at the age of five, it's clear to see why. My mum even told me she'd known since I was 8, and that she'd often wondered if I'd one day want to transition to female – I was particularly fond of her heels. Not to mention that 90% of my friends were female. In fact, one of my closest friends, Harriet and I, decided to become an item. We had a snog in her bedroom and maybe a little bit more, but when it actually came down to… you know… we decided we couldn't go through with it as we both knew what I was. Harriet is still a great friend of mine and is married with two beautiful children.

The next task was to tell my dad, but I couldn't face doing it myself so my mum rang him. There was a lot of yelling going on, and eventually he agreed to come talk to me about it. He came to my mum's house and we began to talk. He blamed my mum for it, saying she had encouraged it by sending me to dance classes. Oh dad, if only it was that easy!

After a very heated discussion, he told me to be ready for 10.30 the next morning. His plan? To take me to a football match. Yes, a football match. I think he was under the misguided illusion that this would somehow cure me of my homosexuality, but I was a hormonal 16 year old watching 22 men in tiny shorts running around a field getting muddy together. It pretty much had the opposite effect.

13 years later… It took a long time, but eventually my dad came round and even apologised for his reaction. Whilst he struggled at first, eventually we got to the point where he classed my partners as part of the family, and even brought one of them on holiday with us.
As for my mum and Pete – they got a feeling of déjà vu when my youngest sister came out to them recently (also at the age of 16!) She's lucky, I did the hard work for her and she had nothing to worry about!

As for me, I broke up with my long term boyfriend a year and a half ago. I'm still getting over it and have no plans to find a boyfriend anytime soon. Instead, I'm going to be travelling the USA for two months to cleanse my mind and reflect on my future, both personally and professionally. Coming out is a terrifying experience, but thankfully things are a lot easier now than they were when I was 16. If your friends and family truly love you, they will always accept you, whatever you are.

And another thing… Whilst coming out is not a mental health issue per se it is nevertheless very stressful for many people to let their loved ones know. Whilst we live in an era where gay and lesbian marriages are widely accepted by many people, society still enforces certain gender identities upon us. Being gay, lesbian, bisexual or transgender is different to the norm and this is where the difficulty lies for many people who want to come out of the closet.

Coming out is a very personal process and some people decide to do this very subtly and gradually whilst others decide to just go through with it and face their family, friends, workplace or school. People can often feel very scared and isolated, unsure about how family and friends may respond and spend a lot of time being anxious around this.

It is ironic that we don't need to approach our parents to tell them we realised that we are heterosexual and we like people of the opposite sex. This is what society is in general expecting of us. So, no need to share that with the rest of the world as it is a given! Being gay or lesbian is a totally different scenario. Having to share our sexual orientation with family and friends is sharing very private and personal information about ourselves. We are not sure about how family and friends will respond. Will they be warm and accepting or will we meet rejection and shame. Coming out can be a very risky business and it is important to choose the right moment. Sometimes people we tell have to get used to the idea and they need a little time.

Coming out is important as keeping your sexual orientation secret can create a lot of stress, it may alienate you from family and friends as you may try to keep it hidden which may necessitate you being secretive and telling lies. Coming out is being true to yourself, accepting who you are and feeling comfortable in your own skin.

Whilst we live in an era where gay and lesbian marriages are widely accepted by many people, society still enforces certain gender identities upon us.

Trevor
Health anxiety

Hi I am Trevor and I am 62 years old. I am married and have three grown up children and two grandchildren and I am three years away from retiring. To be honest, I can't wait! My aching bones are simply begging to stay in bed in the mornings. I actually think it could be a touch of rheumatism. Probably runs in the family as I remember my mother moaning and groaning constantly about her joints playing her up! Come to think of it, my dad always seemed to have a bad back, he was always complaining that it was a definite weak spot or his 'Achilles heel' as he liked to call it!

As for me, mine is my stomach; the acid reflux I get is just awful! Especially if I eat fry ups, which I know are definitely not healthy but I absolutely love them. I even bought one of those 'multi-chefs' that can cook a whole English breakfast in one pan! You just throw everything in: bacon, sausages, egg, mushrooms, tomatoes, and hash browns and 'Voila!' There you have it! That's our weekend treat – both days of course! My wife and I sit in the conservatory and put the world to rights. Enjoying breakfast with a lovely cup of tea, followed by some fresh coffee from our Barista coffee machine. Mind you, I can't drink too much of the stuff as it gives me palpitations. Have you ever had them? How scary are they! Thump thump thump goes my heart, and if I look in the mirror, I can sometimes see my pulse on my neck and my temple! The veins seem to almost bulge out of my head – I wonder if that is normal? I must remember to ask the doctor when I am next down the surgery.

Actually, I should really make an appointment to see someone as I have this weird rash on my left leg. It is probably nothing but it's always better to have it checked out. Whilst I'm there, I should tell the doctor that I would like a memory test. My memory has been dreadful lately! Can you believe that the other day, I put the car keys in my filing tray, instead of my coat pocket and it took me half an hour to find them. I never do that! As for names, don't even get me started! Oh my goodness! I called my new secretary Susan, but her name is April – absolutely no link between those names at all! I do worry a lot about Alzheimer's. I watched 'Still Alice' with my wife the other day, the film is all about some woman getting early onset of Alzheimer's. Now, let me think...who was the actress playing her? I'm sure it was Julie, Jenny or something similar beginning with J. You see, this is what I'm on about, I mean, wouldn't you worry? So yes, I want to have one of those memory tests where they make you draw a clock by hand, they carry on by asking you a series of questions such as 'what year or what month it is?'or 'who the prime minister is?' I must see about getting one booked.

I can't wait to spend more quality time with my wife Ellen. We are already planning to go on a cruise, although no doubt, we will probably spend most of our time throwing up with sea-sickness! We must see the doctor before we go and ensure we get some motion sickness tablets. Hopefully they should alleviate that! Wish he could prescribe some tablets to prevent food poisoning, cruise ships are notorious for spreading Noroviruses! Oh and while I'm thinking about it, I also need to get some anti-histamines, Imodium, paracetamol, a little first-aid kit and some other bits together. Oh, and an EpiPen, you can't ever be sure what will sting you, or what you're allergic to! I definitely need to write a list before my next visit to my GP. I'm forever forgetting to ask him things. I never asked him why my right toe keeps going numb when I do my regular Sunday afternoon walk with my friends. We walk about 15kms, come rain or shine. I enjoy it immensely but my toe keeps going numb. You hear all kinds of stories about people who have MS and they have these weird kind of symptoms. I wonder how MS is diagnosed? Maybe my forgetfulness is to do with that, too! And I am always tired lately.

Have booked this coming Wednesday off. I have to attend the funeral of a colleague. He was only sixty-four and died of some weird cancer, just four months before he was due to retire. Four months! He looked as fit as a fiddle and then suddenly, he felt a little unwell. Anyway, he went to the doctor for some tests a few months ago and was basically told to put his affairs in order! As you can expect, we were all totally shocked! He took time off work for his treatment and he never came back. A few short months, that's all it took! It shook me up, I can tell you! It keeps going through my mind and has really unnerved me.

I have been putting off the bowel cancer check-up. I threw away the test kit that they sent through the post, that must have been a couple of years ago and I've done nothing about it since. The thought of sending off my poo is too embarrassing for words! Also, I'd be terrified if they found anything sinister but think I will get one and have it done, after all, better to be safe than sorry! I have been a little constipated lately and I am usually as regular as clockwork, so there must be something not quite right. There is a lot of bowel cancer about. Maybe I need to have one of those Colo...what's it called? Oh, I just can't think! I know it ends with an 'oscopy!' You simply cannot be too careful these days. One minute you're happily going about your life, and the next, you're dead!

I might actually go to one of those private hospitals and have an all over check-up. You know the ones. They test your blood for every illness going! I think I may even be calcium-deficient and that's why my bones ache every morning. And I have white spots on my finger nails. I will write down all the things I constantly worry about. I don't mind paying for that. I mean, what price do you put on your health!

Six months later... We have had the most amazing cruise. Neither of us got sea sick. We did not even notice the boat moving most of the time! I decided not to go for the health check as it was a lot of money when I asked and my doctor talked me out of it. He explained that the NHS would look after me very well and that I should just do my bowel cancer screening test. He checked my prostate, my blood pressure and my pulse. He also said that he wants me to have a thorough blood test screening for liver function, cholesterol and lots of other things. I went back to see him for a follow up appointment and he actually told me I am as fit as a fiddle! All the tests came back normal. However, he suggested I see one of their counsellors as he believes I worry too much about my health and talking this through with someone would help. I worried about this but eventually saw a lady who helped me see that some of my fears are deep-rooted from my childhood, you know the things that would scare you as a child, or whilst you were growing up. My mother was a terrible worrier and constantly fussed over me. She would keep me off school if I had the slightest hint of a sniffle, thinking it was something worse such as Pneumonia! Because of this, I was an anxious, negative child, always thinking the worst. The counsellor explained that these worries we have, become learnt thinking patterns that manifest themselves in your brain and so the fears and anxieties continue into adulthood. I am currently working on challenging my irrational fears about becoming ill. The counsellor is helping me re-learn better ways of looking at my health in general.

And another thing... We should all try to live healthily and focus on looking after ourselves as much as we can. Watching our weight, staying within safe recommended limits for alcohol and not smoking are a good place to start along with regular exercise and sufficient sleep. But what if we tick all these boxes, yet still worry excessively about our health?

Having concerns about our health is sensible to a point but worrying to the extent where it interferes with our daily life is most likely evidence of health anxiety. It can be quite disruptive to our day to day functioning if we worry that a tummy ache could be stomach cancer, or that we will have a stroke because we have experienced palpitations and a headache.

When we suffer from health anxiety we may be constantly concerned about our body, vigilantly watching out for symptoms that fit the pattern of this or that disease. We may research symptoms looking for evidence that we are ill and make frequent visits to the doctor or unnecessary trips to A and E.

It can also work the opposite way where we try not to come into contact with ill people, desperately avoiding hospitals and doctors' surgeries. But generally we read more into the slightest symptoms we experience. So an episode of cystitis will most likely be seen as bladder cancer, and acid reflux must surely be stomach cancer.

People with health anxiety often catastrophise and worry about what will happen to their loved ones when they die. They may seek constant reassurance from not just health professionals but from their family and friends. They may sometimes behave as though they already have the particular illness they fear, and there may be avoidance of certain activities that are perceived as carrying risk, for example going on holiday, or flying.

For some people, the roots of health anxiety lie in childhood. They may have copied a parent or family member, believing it to be the right way to think about health. Or perhaps they were on the receiving end of excessive worry about their health from a family member, resulting in the belief that there must be good reason to be concerned. There may have been a family member who had, or still has, a serious health condition. Or there could have been a death in the family caused by a major disease.

If health anxiety has become a major issue that is difficult to manage, talking therapies can help. In particular Cognitive Behavioural Therapy (CBT) has proved to be quite effective as it helps to challenge dysfunctional thinking patterns.

Patrick
Self harm

Hi, I am Patrick and I am 19 years old. I recently attended an interview at an art college in Leeds and have now been told I have an unconditional offer for September. Needless to say, I am absolutely over the moon!

My parents are delighted too, so much so that they have given me £100 to treat myself. What a life saver that is! I can finally book myself in with my tattooist to fill in that last bit on my right arm. Both my arms are a piece of art, all my own artwork! Not quite Picasso, I don't quite put myself in his category but I'm not half bad, even if I do say so myself! I designed what I wanted the tattooist to put on my arms and I don't even want to think about how much money I have spent over the years. I love my tattoos but they are actually there to hide the evidence... No, I am not Michael Scofield from Prison Break. There is no secret map depicting hidden tunnels and underground passageways on my arms, to get me out of prison. Ironically, they hide my self-inflicted wounds, the scars of emotional imprisonment from my past. You see, I am a self-harmer! Well, I used to be. When things were bad and the pressure in my head was insurmountable, I would cut my arms to pieces in a bid to release my anger and all the pent up emotions inside me. You know what I am talking about? When you literally feel your head is on the absolute verge of exploding! What would it even look like if your head exploded? There's a video on YouTube of a watermelon being dropped from a high-rise building - I imagine it would look something like that! Yuck! It's not a pleasant sight or thought!

To tell you the truth, I don't even know how it all started or what it was all about. During my early teens, I seemed to be insanely angry, hating everyone and everything! Maybe it was because my parents split up when I was much younger and subconsciously, I don't feel I ever got over it. I am not really sure why I was so angry. It wasn't like I woke up one day, thinking "Today, I'm going to be really angry and hate the world and all who live in it!" But, looking back, it was so hard to express how I felt, so for me, the only way I could let go of my emotions and feelings, was to carve my arms up! I wanted, no, needed that release, as without it, the pressure was unbearable. Also it was a way of having some control over how I felt. It helped to quieten the turmoil and rage inside my head.

I never really talked to anyone about it. I could have cut other parts of my body, one of my flatmates at uni used to cut her arms, thighs and her stomach. For me, I needed to see the blood trickling down my arms and feel the warmth of it as it made its scarlet rivulets on my skin. The relief was instant and gratifying! Immediately after, I would tell myself I needed to stop as my arms were becoming so scarred, but when the pressure built up, I had to have that release! In the winter, it was easy to hide the 'evidence' under my school shirts and jumper, but summer was not so easy. Along with the warm weather, summer would bring heightened levels of stress and anxiety – how would I cover my arms? God, how I despised those hot summer days! Have you ever tried to sit in your dad's garden, when the thermometer is showing 32 degrees Celsius, in the shade! (Joking!) Imagine it, you're sitting there, wearing a long-sleeved top, the sweat is pouring from you, your hair is sticking to your head, and everyone around you is adorned in an array of summer tops, with tanned arms on display. I remember my dad, who was unaware of my scars, would shout "Patrick, take your top off! And then at regular intervals, "For God's Sake, Patrick, did you not hear me? He would then mumble to anyone who cared to listen, how he just did not understand teenagers! I swear I almost died a thousand deaths in that garden, each time, coming dangerously close to a heat stroke before I stumbled inside looking for salvation and shade! How I yearned to join my nephews and nieces, as they splashed about in the paddling pool.

My mum found out eventually. To be fair, she was great and offered to listen and encouraged me to talk to her about it but I just could not. But from that point onwards, whenever I came home from high school, she ensured there was always some TCP antiseptic, an assortment of plasters, and bandages that were easily accessible. Aren't mums just so practical! I half expected her to place them in a pot and label it! I would panic that she had been in my room and found the blades hidden in one of my drawers, but they were always there; never taken away. She probably realised that there was no point, as I would have just used something else, something that was not that clean! Her reasoning must have been that, at least the wound would be relatively clean and neat.

One day, one of my close friends at the time, saw my scars, as I was changing my sweater. I had stupidly spilt some coke on it and without thinking, pulled it off my arms and straight over my head. He seemed really shocked and asked me if I was trying to kill myself. Of course that was not the case at all but I tried to make a joke of it and explain it to him, as simply as I could but it scared him and he never mentioned it again. Thinking back, had he done so, I would have opened up about it all, to him. At that time, I was quite alone with all my emotions, and as a grown man now, I realise that I could have talked to my parents about it all and more importantly, I would have received an understanding and supportive response. Unfortunately, at the time, it just did not feel like that for me.

People are too quick to judge by far and often think self-harmers are trying to kill themselves, or that they are attention seekers! They are just keen to slap a label on it, and you know, they are just so wrong!! What if I told you that self-harm has the nickname 'Silent Scream?' There you go! That describes it perfectly! That's what I often felt like doing but instead of screaming out, I screamed silently inside and it was painful, and the only way I could feel that pain, was by cutting. It is so far removed from wanting to die, I never wanted to die, I just could not cope with my emotional turmoil and confusion. I desperately needed to express it all but I was just so scared to do so.

And how could self-harming even be attention seeking when people try very hard to hide their scars or they cut themselves or burn themselves in places that are usually hidden? They also usually do it in the privacy of their bedroom, so how can that be attention seeking? If I really wanted to seek attention, there are far easier ways, believe me! Why, it would take me seconds to strip off and run down the street, screaming! That would definitely attract attention!

Obviously, I now have a much better understanding of what I was doing and I know for sure that I never really wanted to frighten or manipulate anyone, least of all my parents! It was more of a desperate act, a way of trying to communicate my inside feelings but without being able to. It was also quite methodical and would always result in me taking the blades and injuring myself. The pain just had to come out somehow. I failed to verbalise it, so I bled it out! I really wanted to scream and shout but instead of that, I totally internalised my anger and then the pressure always got too much. So many times I just felt powerless and helpless, and very much alone with all my emotions. Wow! Did I just really say all that? There you go, that was all very clear, wasn't it?! I so wish I could have expressed myself that well in those early years. I may never have injured myself. Who knows! I must say, I've found it extremely therapeutic to write all this down, who would have guessed I could remember it all so well!

12 years later... All that was a long time ago and now I have other outlets. I run my own business based on various art projects. In a way, my creativity has also been my savior, and not surprisingly, I have chosen a career where I can use this creativity to the full. I am now a married man with children, I am also a home owner and have a wide circle of really interesting friends who are also into the same sort of arty stuff.

I am also volunteering for a Self-Harm website, where I moderate some of the contributions members of the public make. My role is to censor all unsuitable or potentially damaging contributions, people sometimes make.

And another thing... Self-harm has been called a Silent Scream. People who self-harm are not attention seeking. Nor do they have a death wish. It is a way of trying to stop difficult and distressing emotions. It may sometimes become life-threatening and require hospital treatment (e.g. a wound could become infected or a cut be deep enough to require stitches).

Self-harm can encompass many things such as cutting parts of your body, pulling hair, picking and scratching skin, deliberately breaking bones or taking risks with your health, ingesting poisonous substances or deliberately burning yourself.

Self-harming can often be about survival and the only way some people can cope with life from day to day. It can also be a form of self-punishment when a person feels guilt or shame about events in their life.

Often it is the only way a person can manage their emotions and cope with the intense pressure and stress that has built up inside. For others, who feel emotionally numb, it is the only way they can "feel", for example, sensing the warm blood running down their arm. It is worth mentioning here that sometimes the body produces natural opiates and the process of cutting may, in these cases, not be too physically painful to the person.

Self-harm may be an attempt to communicate to the outside world that something is wrong that the person cannot verbally express, often due to extremely low self-esteem and sense of worth.

It is frightening seeing someone self-harming and people often feel helpless, as they don't know how to respond. Perhaps the most important thing to remember is not to ask the person to stop self-harming. Instead, listening to them, guiding the person to professional help (talking therapies or seeing their GP), perhaps encouraging them to delay the urge to self-harm by ten minutes or so to see if they still feel the need, finding a support group or useful website with a forum or encouraging them to express their emotions by being creative may all be helpful.

Providing information on self-harm, telephone numbers of helplines and helping the person to expand their support network may also be a positive step. Along with suggestions such as keeping a diary, writing poetry, making a scrapbook, painting or playing an instrument, which may help to express or release emotion.

When supporting someone who self-harms it is important to access support yourself as the emotions it brings up may be difficult to handle on your own.

Owen

Anger issues

Hi my name is Owen. You don't need to know my age because quite frankly, it is none of your damn business! What's it to you? People are far too nosy these days! Did I ask you how old you are? No? Exactly!

I am sick and tired of people always trying to get at me, the whole world seems to have gone mad! Honestly, I tell you, from the minute I get up, it begins! There's my damn alarm clock for starters! I'm still tired, it is cold and miserable and I have no wish to surface and face the day! How I hate the winter months! The low temperatures, grey mornings, grey days... makes me so grumpy. Then there's the cat! I daren't turn over in bed or make the slightest noise, as it starts her off, a constant whining mewing as she begs to be fed. Such an incessant high-pitched noise, I can't stand it so early in the day!

So I finally get my breakfast and go to make a cup of tea, and guess what? Yes, the the milk is off! I threw the contents of my mug away and then realise I have not put enough water in the kettle to make another cup, so go through the whole procedure again...fill the kettle, boil the kettle, then proceed to make a cup of tea without milk. Yuck! I like my builders' tea in the mornings. To have it without milk is disgusting! Why can't my wife make sure there is fresh milk in the fridge? I mean, it doesn't take an Einstein now, does it!

So I drive to work and par for the course, every single learner driver, within a ten-mile radius seems to be out this time of day! Why can't they have their lessons outside of rush hour? Am I the only one who that makes sense to? Oops, here we go, yet another driver who thinks they're exempt from using indicators! You would think that someone dropping their child off at school, would set a good example by ensuring they signal that they are pulling over, but then again, she is a woman driver! Bloody women! Should never be allowed on the roads! Winding the window down, I ask her: "indicator broken love? No? Then bloody well use it in future, you gormless bitch! I nearly crashed into you." I zoom off a little faster than I wanted but I was really angry with her.

I pull into the car park at work and see that some inconsiderate and obviously illiterate person has parked in my spot. I mean, who in their right mind would even have the audacity to park in a space that clearly states it is "Reserved for O. Jenkins?" Fuming doesn't even come close to it! Now I have to park right at the end of the car park and it is raining for God's sake! I hate the rain!

The day continues on the same path it began on. Upon reaching my office, I find my PA has already let Andrew into my office. He is one of my top ten customers and I can't stand him! Arrogant prick! Thinks he knows it all! Robert, the sales manager and Mike, our production manager join us. A two-hour meeting and it really does not go so well! Andrew is unhappy with the last few deliveries of 'Masterbatches' and makes no bones about telling us! We have had a few complaints recently from some of our much smaller account holders but Andrew complaining is a big deal! Our regular supplier for some of the additives, closed down their production and we had to change suppliers. To be perfectly honest, the quality of their products is just not up to scratch, and now our customers are not happy at all. Andrew says that the latest deliveries are just not blending so well and are affecting the colours of the end products. Andrew's company make high-end plastic bags and plastic boxes and his customers are unhappy. So the ultimatum he gives us is that we either sort it out or he will be forced to look elsewhere. Although I detest him, it would definitely be an account I would be ----unhappy to lose. He spends about £280,000 per year with us and heads will roll if we lose him!

I walk him down to reception and we look at the grim weather. "Lousy day!" I say to him, in a bid to diffuse the slightly frosty atmosphere. As he shakes my hand and walks towards the car park, I shout after him: "Hope you're not parked too far away like I had to? Can you believe that some dickhead parked in my slot today!" Ouch! Yes, you got it! You are 100% correct in assuming that Andrew walked over to my parking spot and got into his car!". I caught his eye and gave him an embarrassed grin but was inwardly cursing myself. How could I be so bloody stupid? Hard to believe, but my mood got even worse and consequently everyone pretty much avoided me for the rest of the day! I know I'm having a bad morning and all that but do I actually have a post-it note on my forehead, announcing to all that: "I am totally hacked off with the whole world and I bite" written on my forehead?"

After lunch, I'm sat at my desk, trying to relax with a coffee when the phone goes and I lean forward to answer it, damn! I knock the cup all over my keyboard: "For crying out loud!!" I jump up a little too quickly and jerk my neck awkwardly! Pain radiates down my spine. Clearly the whole world is against me today! In a rage, I grab the nearest thing, and throw it as hard as I can... I stand there in disbelief as my new iPhone 7 lies there with the screen totally shattered on the floor! At this point, I could literally scream! My face is hot, I'm feeling uncomfortable and palpitations are surging through my body. (I keep getting those lately and yet I am physically fit and healthy. I play squash regularly. God knows I need to have an outlet in this job. But I find I can really let off steam in the squash court! It gets my adrenalin pumping and I feel ready for anything afterwards. It's fantastic for de-stressing!) I somehow get through the remainder of the afternoon, acutely aware of various stares and whispering throughout the building, whenever I leave the safety of my office. Yes, very funny, Mr Jenkins had a melt-down and smashed his phone! Get over it!

Finally, I leave and get completely soaked on my sprint to the car, I place my briefcase on the back seat, along with some papers I need for tomorrow. Oh, for God's sake! I remember then that my secretary reminded me earlier, it is Valentine's Day. I'll have to nip to the supermarket and try to find some flowers, that's if they still have some left! It seems like everyone has chosen to go food shopping now! "Wait! You're going the wrong way, follow the arrows! You bloody idiot! Oh for goodness sake, that parking space was mine! How selfish! What a stupid arsehole!" Right, that's it. I am parking in the parent and child car park. They have plenty of them. Ok, maybe not that many, but who cares! I will only be five minutes...

"You are joking, £30 for a bunch of roses? What a rip off! That is daylight robbery!" After sounding off, I curse to myself as I realise I have left my wallet at work. It must have been when they did a collection earlier today for Mavis's retirement fund... I think I put it in my drawer instead of back in my pocket. Bloody Mavis! Ah well, not to worry, I'll do an online payment on my phone instead. Shit! More realisation, as I think back to my earlier outburst and the mental image of my trashed iPhone comes into focus. God! Is anything going to go right today? That's going to go down like a lead balloon tonight! Should have taken her out for a meal really, I just did not think.

Oh my goodness! Look at that idiot buying chocolates, roses and a bottle of Prosecco! He'll be in for a good night! Yeah, well make the most of it, mate! It doesn't last! I'll give it ten years, a couple of kids, a mortgage round your neck and an ungrateful wife with endless demands. See if you buy her that bunch then!

Shaking my head at my predicament and the soppy guy at the next checkout, I walk empty-handed back to my car Oh you're joking! What's he doing with my car? Hang on, that's not a policeman, it's a parking attendant and he is writing out a ticket. Shaking with rage, I storm up to him: "What on earth do you think you're doing? I have literally been five minutes, mate. Do you really have to?"

"Sir, I'm afraid we have zero tolerance for people abusing the rules in the car park. I cannot see a child seat in your car, and neither are you with a child at this moment. Now, if you can prove otherwise, I will be more than happy to tear the ticket up but other than that..."

"Yeah, yeah, someone sticks you in a uniform and you think you own the place! Well, stuff you and stuff your stupid rules, you bloody wanker!"

"Sean, I need assistance, and get someone to call the police? We've got a right one here!"

Ten months later... After the altercation with the parking attendant (that ended up turning into a physical brawl) Owen ended up in court. He was fined £400 and 80 hours community service. That was quite a bitter pill to swallow and extremely humiliating when the other directors found out. In fact the whole company knew.

He was also ordered to attend a course of six anger management sessions where he learnt better and safer ways of expressing anger. Whilst looking at his anger, he realised where some of it stemmed from and found ways of dealing with trigger situations better. It also dawned on him that he had not taken a holiday for eight months due to heavy work commitments, and that he was doing paperwork most weekends as well as every evening during the week. He stopped playing squash, as during his anger management treatment, it was suggested he attend calmer activities such as mindfulness or meditation classes instead. Owen also started to go to work half an hour earlier to beat the school traffic, and would use that time to deal with all the paperwork he would normally carry out at home. This freed most of his evenings to enjoy with his family.

He lost Andrew as a customer and sadly as a result of this, the company had to let three people go. He finally managed to find a better supplier of 'masterbatches' and now enjoys his interaction with the other major customers, taking them out for a relaxed business lunch and the odd round of golf! Owen's Facebook page is filled with photos showing him enjoying a family holiday in Barbados. Life is now so much better!

And another thing... Anger is sometimes described as stress (or distress) in disguise. It is a part of being human and one of the many feelings or emotions we have such as joy, happiness, fear, anxiety and sadness. So we should not always view anger negatively.

A lot of us are familiar with the fight or flight response, a throwback to the Stone Ages where man had to chase after his food. The problem was that sometimes the food itself had fast legs and sharp teeth! So when our ancestors were chasing rabbits, wild cats and snakes to take back to the rest of the tribe, they had to fight to conquer their prey (fight response). However, if the animal were bigger and stronger, the same man would have to run (flight response) to avoid being killed and eaten. In each case the body would undergo physiological changes to prepare itself to either run or to fight, though obviously these changes differed.

While we no longer have to chase our food or be chased by potential food, the fight or flight response mechanisms are still very much part of our make up, only now it is often about perceived threat. Our brain accesses a whole range of stored data comparable to other situations in our memory bank and if there is a perceived threat, the brain differentiates between a significant threat and a milder threat. We react differently depending on how the threat is perceived. This process happens almost instantaneously.

An anger response is then strongly linked to the situations we find ourselves in, and how we see others. And anger is the emotion a lot of us dislike in ourselves and in others as it is considered to be not 'nice'. Yet it is such an important emotion. Anger is a massive topic in its own right and it is very misunderstood as it evokes fear and discomfort. We are therefore often quick to try to dampen it in others. Of course, I don't want to be naïve in thinking that there is not a great deal of pure aggression and totally inappropriately expressed anger out there and it is completely unacceptable. However, the kind of anger I am referring to is the day-to-day anger, which we could learn to express in a less frightening and less intimidating way.

People who decide to go for anger management therapy will often find they have to explore their upbringing and role models within the family set up. The counsellor may wish to find out if as a child the client was encouraged to verbalise anger as well as happier emotions. What were the socialisation messages from earlier in their life? Were they told never to show anger, as it was not nice behaviour? What was their emotional response when anger was expressed towards them by significant others in their lives? They will look at family relationships and how emotions in general were communicated amongst other family members.

An anger management counsellor will look at the client's environment, stress levels, trigger points, level of self-esteem and self-worth, level of self-care, and work / life balance to see when and how they release stress. They may encourage the client to start a regular sport activity or encourage them to use mindfulness or meditation.

Anger is closely linked to the way we think and therapy can help us reframe some of our thinking errors into healthier ways of seeing things. Cognitive Behaviour Therapy can be very helpful in identifying thinking errors but is not the only helpful talking therapy.

There are of course some things you can do before you even access therapy. These include: counting to 30 rather than just 10 (which may not be enough to distract our thought process), walking away, using positive calming self-talk, which is not about saying you are fine when you are not, but rather saying that you are upset; thinking about the consequences if you were to get angry right then, focusing your anger at the problem rather than the person, reducing stress where you can and trying to live a well-balanced life, getting sufficient sleep as lack of sleep makes people irritable, taking responsibility for how you feel, looking at your expectations of people and asking yourself if it is perhaps you who needs to make changes rather than the other person, not jumping to conclusions by adding two and two together and making five, and not talking AT people but instead talking with them.

Also try to reduce the amount of caffeine you take as this can affect our level of agitation. Please note that some extra strong painkillers contain large amounts of caffeine, so always check the label if you are a regular user of this type of medication.

But the main message here is that if you recognise your anger is getting out of hand and is starting to hurt the people you are with, then accessing help and support is important in order to learn better ways of dealing with anger.

Evelyn
Abandonment issues

Hi, my name is Evelyn and I am 48 years old. You want to know what my t-shirt says? It says 'Currently under construction!' That's because I'm soon to be having delayed reconstructive surgery. Don't look so shocked! I am quite looking forward to my operation, it's scheduled sometime in the next few weeks. I will soon be wearing t-shirts and dresses again, no more hiding under cardigans and baggy jumpers!

It all started about 14 months ago, when I was trying bikinis on for my holiday. I noticed a small lump about half a centimetre. I tend to be a bit lumpy, so I did not really think much of it, as I have had several tests in the past and they all came back okay. Anyway, off I jetted to my holiday in the sun, soaking up that much needed sunshine! I completely forgot about the lump and just concentrated on having a good time with my amazing fiancé, Carl. He was such a dish and all mine! Dark curly hair, with just a hint of grey around his temples but it so suited him. Why is it that a bit of grey makes men more interesting or "distinguished," yet we women are 'encouraged' to colour our hair to hide our age? So unfair! Carl had quite a hairy chest, I never realised how hairy it was until I saw him parading around half-naked for most of the holiday. But I have to say, it was so relaxing sitting by his side, both laid on sunbeds, me reading my book... Was it my imagination or was he looking at the girl nearby, who was 'wearing' a green, almost non-existent bikini? I know mine was a little daring for someone my age but it was a couple of years ago and I felt I could pull it off! Anyway, hers was cut away, revealing (or some might say, exposing) an extremely pert rear-end! Wow, I must admit even I took a second glance, but Carl shouldn't have! I thought I looked very attractive in my floral, cerise pink bikini. I even noticed a couple of the waiters staring at me whilst I sipped a late afternoon cocktail on my own. Carl didn't spot them though; he was too busy playing water polo with some other guys he had befriended.

I returned from our holiday, as brown as a berry and feeling even more in love than before. I felt blessed that I had a gorgeous man who wanted to spend the rest of his life with me! Back home and back into my familiar routine, I returned to work and booked a session at the gym.

Adjusting my top, I suddenly felt something... oh my goodness, the lump! It was still there and I was sure it was not that hard before the holidays. Anyway, I thought I better have it checked out, so I went to see the doctor, who said it needed investigating, as it did not feel like a fatty lump this time. I worried myself sick when he said that. Soon after, I had a biopsy, followed by blood tests and an ultrasound scan. They were so thorough, and for that I was grateful but then came the result... Never in a million years was I expecting bad news. I had gone on my own but was dearly wishing that Carl had taken time off to come with me. That night we spoke and he was so supportive. He reassured me that he would go to all future examinations, treatments and he swore that he will be by my side to fight it together...He kept his promise and came along to all my appointments and was there right next to me, when it was suggested that I have a double mastectomy... He squeezed my hand real tight at that point and I felt so supported and loved. "Thank God, you are in my life! I know I can get through anything, with you by my side!" I told him.

Weeks and months passed and I carried on having regular treatments for my cancer. We delayed our wedding plans until after my planned reconstructive surgery. I did not want to walk down the aisle without breasts! It was as simple as that!

Soon after, my best friend rang me, it was early in the morning and I thought it strange as she didn't usually ring then. Anyway, she asked if she could have breakfast with me as she had taken the day off. Cool, I thought! Would be great to spend some time with her. A girlie day! Long time since I had one of those. I was still on sick leave as I felt so rough and nauseous with the treatment. As I was making breakfast, she dropped the bombshell. She explained that she had been in a café, and was sitting outside, when she suddenly spotted Carl with a very young lady and her fluffy dog. Carl and the girl were holding hands and my friend, Sharon had taken a photo on her phone to show me. My heart pounding, I studied the photo, there was no mistake, it was him. I looked more intently at the girl...Oh my God, I knew her! It was his previous lodger, a young student who had moved over from Nottingham.

Consequently, I am no longer engaged. I obviously confronted Carl that evening and showed him the photo my friend had forwarded to me. He did not even try to deny or apologise. He said he wanted to tell me, but did not know how because I was ill. He admitted he struggled with my diagnosis and went on rather cruelly to say he did not want to marry a woman who had no breasts. As blunt as that! I screamed at him that I was having reconstructive surgery soon. "Yes, he shouted back. "But they would be fake and it is not the same!" That same evening, he packed his stuff and left and I never saw him again. Literally, life sucked then! Talk about feeling low and feeling incredibly unfeminine! What had he done to me? Because of that lousy rat, I had to have counselling for months after! But you know, looking back, I can clearly see that I had a lucky escape by not marrying him. Talking things through in counselling, gave me a massive insight.

Throughout my adult years I have had four relationships in total. Whilst at uni, I was with Tom. He dabbled with drugs and was a lazy, laid-back kind of guy. I missed so many lectures because he would persuade me to spend the day in bed eating Ben & Jerry's and watching crap like Jerry Springer, but then he left me for the girl who did his tattoos. I'm guessing the discount he no doubt got from then on, was a massive incentive!

Then there was Stewart, a journalist who wrote for The Sunday Sport at the time. Thank goodness it no longer exists! It was just the trashiest of all papers! In hindsight, I should have known that we were not going to last, but I just did not see it coming! He was so good looking and had a huge appetite in the bedroom department! So much so, that I apparently couldn't satisfy his hunger pangs! For one day, I walked in on him and my housemate! I had left a course early, due to a tummy bug and obviously was not expected home then! It was difficult to say who was more shocked but I know who shouted the loudest! There were major changes that week! The house belonged to me. I put down a deposit on it, when my parents kindly gave me a share of their inheritance from my grandparents. Shelley, my 'delightful' housemate was originally a friend of a friend who came to live with me. It suited us both, I had a spare bedroom, she needed a place to stay and the rent money helped me pay the mortgage. Up to then she was good fun, but having fun with my boyfriend was not part of the deal! Cheeky cow! So I lost my boyfriend, my housemate (and extra income) and my job that month! You see, I was working at the same company as Stewart, who had transferred over to my more respected newspaper company. But it was too painful to work within the same building plus it didn't go down well with my bosses that I spent a considerable time that week, in the ladies' toilet, crying my eyes out, so I handed my notice in.

Then there was Graham, my boss! That was a huge mistake! I thought I would go for a change, an older man - as men my age always seemed to let me down! Ha! Don't make me laugh! Graham promised for months that he would leave his wife, as there was 'nothing left between them'. He would constantly reel off that the only connection they had was their two children but nothing else and went on to say that they were even sleeping in separate bedrooms and had been for some time. Imagine my shock when I overheard Adrian, the co-director of the company, congratulating Stewart on the forthcoming arrival of his third child! Putting the coffees on the table, I visibly shook as I spilt the contents of one mug. 'Separate bedrooms?' yeah, right! What was it then? Immaculate conception!

Composing myself, I walked into his office. Stewart began spluttering excuses... "I was going to tell you today, honestly. I did not want you to hear it this way... in view of the circumstances, I think we had better... Ignoring his waffle, I placed my letter of resignation on his table and curtly told him I would be leaving that day and would not be working my notice. That was the very least he owed me! I never saw him again either but I hope he drowned in shitty nappies!

So, in a nutshell, that is the story of my life. Men enter my life and then suddenly disappear. No warning, no easing me into it gently, just buggering off out of my life as if I have some smelly disease. What was so wrong that I could not keep a man? Was I that bad, that unlovable?

Six months later... My brilliant counsellor listened to my story, my tears, my rage, my self-pitying lamenting pleas of things that needed to change. Gradually she made me realise that what I was doing, was replaying the actual story of my life, time and time again. Why had I not seen it? It was crystal clear when I unpicked it all in therapy. I went right back to my early childhood and realised that I was damaged very early on. It happened when I was about five. My father came into the yard where my sister and I were playing. She was three years younger than me. He gave me a hug and a kiss and told me he needed to leave and that I was his big girl and should look after my mum and my sister for him. I never saw him again. He literally abandoned us!

We had a hard life and my poor mum had to work several jobs to keep us warm and fed. Occasionally, she would bring a man into our lives for short periods of time, but one by one she kicked them out, until one day she stopped bringing them home. I did find my real dad about eight years ago on Facebook, when a friend introduced me to it. I invited him to be my friend but he declined the request. I was still able to see some of the photos he had posted. There were some of him sat with a couple of toddlers and a young woman, who looked like she was in her late 30's. I wondered and imagined scenarios of who they were to him. We sadly never met but when attending a family funeral, I found out through a distant relative, that he had left my mum for another woman and had remarried and had two further children with this woman. A boy and a girl. The children in the photo were actually his grandchildren. Grandchildren? Can you believe that!

As I showed my counsellor all the photos, I sobbed and I sobbed. I must have emptied her box of tissues! The realisation of what I was consistently acting out on the stage of my adult life, was the same scenario I experienced that sunny morning, when my dad told me he was leaving. Consequently, that is what I was replaying with every man I chose. You see, the script was already written at the beginning of every relationship I embarked upon. To simplify it, I subconsciously went for rats who would inevitably do something to sabotage the relationship.

Making that massive connection between the abandonment I experienced in my childhood and replaying the abandonment in my adult relationships, helped me break the self-destructive spell! I'm delighted to say that the light bulbs are well and truly on now!
So I look forward to having reconstructive surgery and after my recovery from that, I will see what the future holds for me in terms of any relationships I may embark upon. But one thing is for certain, it will be on my newly-acquired terms!

And another thing... Abandonment happens in childhood. This can be because a parent may have passed away or parents decided to get divorced. However, abandonment can also happen when a child may have been with both parents throughout their childhood but poor parenting may have occurred, maybe in the form of unattainable pressure and expectations or the child being ridiculed or made the scapegoat of everyone else's shortcomings. Abandonment can also happen if a child was emotionally, physically or sexually abused, thus representing a very unsafe and traumatising childhood. It could also be that some of the very basic needs such as adequate shelter, heat or food were not provided. Some children are damaged in this way by parents leaning on them for emotional support or seeing the child more as their friend. This sense of aloneness and desperation can result in children growing up as adults with very poor self-esteem and feeling worthless.

As adults with those kinds of ideas about self we can subconsciously get locked into cycles of connecting with other humans who are most unsuitable. This will often result in these connections breaking down, thus replaying the abandonment we felt as a child. As adults we can play these issues out over and over again without realising that we keep pressing the rewind and play buttons for the same scenario being acted out again and again, often with different people.

Talking therapies can help a person stop the patterns they are repeating by differentiating what belongs in the past and what should remain in the current or future stage of a person's life. Therapy can help the person look at ways of increased self-care, help them set safe and healthy boundaries, help them identify their needs and how to express these within intimate and personal relationships and how to learn to trust others, knowing that they are now in control of their own destiny as the replay function has been permanently switched off.

Talking therapies can help a person stop the patterns they are repeating by differentiating what belongs in the past and what should remain in the current or future stage of a person's life.

Isla

Anxiety

Hi, my name is Isla and I am 20 years old. I suffer from Anxiety and here is my story. I think it is important to tell you this story as some of my friends are surprised I had "issues" with anxiety when I have such a loving family around me and live a fairly normal life. I live with my mum, my dad and my sister in a big house, I have lots of amazing friends, I love fashion and music and cocktails. My life is quite well balanced I would say....... So you wonder why I of all people should suffer anxiety?

Well, it all started a long time ago. My grandparents live at the seaside. And every summer my sister and I were excited about going there and spending a week with them. We couldn't wait and counted the days each summer from breaking up until the day we drove down in the car. Three hour journey where we both made it our mission to drive our parents mad with non-stop singing along to a playlist we prepared together for each trip.

The best trips of all where the Christmas trips when my dad used to sing along totally out of tune! Fairy tale of New York was the one where he sounded the worst! Yes, dad, don't give up your day job, whatever you do!

I must have been around 10 years old when mum wanted to visit family abroad and suggested my dad, my sister and I go and visit our grandparents for a week. We were chuffed to go on a car journey just with dad as he would turn the music right up and actually try and sing along with us although he messed up the words in every song! I totally forgot to tell you that my auntie and her family live two doors away from my grandparents and we were always so excited about seeing our three cousins. They are all boys but great fun! Always teasing us and stuff but in a fun kind of way, so we really did not mind.

Our favourite thing of all has always been hitting the arcades. Dad and Auntie Stacey decided we should hop in her car and she would take us all down. She had a big car with seven seats. I loved sitting right at the back pulling faces at the cars behind us or better still betting how many people will wave back at us. Now that was something I always won! Must have had that irresistible charm, you know!

Si (my older cousin) and I always played air hockey whilst the others tried to get as many tickets as possible from different machines. The air hockey game that day was a really good long game! He beat me at the last minute so I put some more money in and begged him for a rematch. This time I wanted to win!! It was so exciting! I needed the loo but had no idea if the arcades had toilets. I would ask Dad in a bit, after the game. The game started and I was so focussed on trying to win. But my side began to hurt a little bit. Si kept saying he is going to beat me again and I was even more determined to win... Until I totally froze!! I stopped moving altogether and must have had a very strange look on my face as Si's face changed. He looked puzzled and lifted his arms as if to say "What?!"

My thighs suddenly went very warm as I could feel my wee trickle down my legs. I desperately tried to stop the flow but I couldn't. I just burst out crying and managed to whimper "Get my dad please. Quick. Get my dad!" Dad came running and there was no need for him to be told what happened. He could see the dark patches on my jeans. I well and truly had wet my pants with the excitement of the game and I was frozen to the spot with total horror and embarrassment. Thankfully, the air hockey table was in a darkish corner away from most machines. Si was not really sure what was going on and Dad asked him to get his jacket from the coffee lounge where he and Aunty Stacey were having a coffee. Dad wrapped it around my legs and then scooped me up and walked into the coffee lounge. He asked Auntie Stacey to get up and get the others and walked ahead to the car park.

Longest journey ever back to gran's house and by that time I was crying and frankly I was scared. Not sure why really. Dad did not shout at me, neither did gran. But I was just in a state of shock I guess as this had never happened before. Gran ran me a bath and sorted some clean clothes for me and I was eternally grateful having the "bestest Gran in the world".

Winding forward to the present day toilets have taken on a significant meaning in my life. In fact I was thrilled to have used the highest toilet in Paris, on the Eiffel Tower no less! That was on a family trip to Paris. Any journeys for me are closely intertwined with the need to know where my next wee is going to be and how soon I will get there. Being trapped in a car or on public transport is just the worst scenario for me. I am still a little OCD about it all as I have to insist we stop at each service station. Mum always had to have a discreet word about me to the teachers before going on any school trips to make sure there are plenty of toilet stops. Then came my final year of our A levels and as an A level art student I was going on a five day art trip to the south of England along the coast. The teacher told us to pack our swim wear as the weather was scorching hot and we would be given opportunity to swim. "We have five hours at a secluded beach with excellent coast line to draw and paint. No tourists. Just us" he announced! Everyone cheered! I just thought "Oh damn, no toilet, male teacher and just sand all around. How am I supposed to do that? I mean, I don't mind going behind the bushes and all that but on a secluded beach there ARE no bushes! I went quiet. "See you all Monday morning, don't be late!"

Sunday morning came and I woke up very miserable. Packing my bag I noticed my hands were shaking. Ten pm came and I burst into the lounge in tears and told my parents I am not able to go on the trip. "But we paid £185 for it and we can't cancel now!" "I just can't go" I said over and over again. "I realise it is a problem and I now know that I need help with this, mum" I pleaded desperately.

She drove me to school and had a word with my art teacher explaining what the issue is. He came over and reassured me it is ok and off they went. I was just so relieved. And I stayed with another class that week at school.

When I got home mum told me she made an appointment for me to see someone and although all these years I insisted I am okay after what happened with this cancelling the trip even I had to admit that I definitely should talk to someone. So I went along and this counsellor did a mixture of hypnotherapy and counselling in the first session. I was so tense that I started to cry in the first ten minutes. The hypnotherapy just relaxed me initially. To my big surprise she did not send me into a trance where I was not in possession of my full faculties, not at all as you see on the telly where people make a spectacle of themselves and then cannot remember. She was not kidding when she said to me that I will stay in control whilst under hypnosis, and I was. I told her that any trip, even a trip to school or a shopping trip was a major issue as I had to do this ritual of going to the toilet before I go. And now I am at uni sometimes this meant I missed a train! It was that bad! Honestly!

Going to the seaside to visit my grandparents is a three hour trip and guess what! Yep! You guessed correctly. Three trips to the loo, one trip for each hour. AND: I have to always be the last person going to the loo before leaving the house! Okay, that is extreme, I know! But, such is the extent of my anxiety! So you can see why I needed a bit of extra help with this whole issue.

Four months later... I am much better generally with anxiety not just around toilets but generally speaking. My lovely counsellor has not just used hypnotherapy to get me relaxed on a deeper level but in subsequent sessions she taught me EFT (Emotional Freedom Technique) which is a tapping therapy. You have to tap certain points on your head, face and upper body and say stuff and sing and count backwards and all that but actually, oddly enough it just takes the anxiety away generally. Not only do I no longer get anxious when I go on trips nowadays but the tapping thing really helps with exam nerves and lately even my interviews at uni! It is a skill I can keep using in the future and no doubt I will have many anxious moments where it will be useful! I am now also an avid reader of novels as I realised that losing myself in a good book is a great way to relax.

And another thing... Anxiety is fear. It is a mixture of physical and psychological symptoms brought about by a perceived threat, not an actual one. It can be very distressing and can grow the more we think about it and focus on it.

People can suffer from anxiety for various reasons: it can be in our genetic make-up or be due to an early life experience (as in the example of Isla having wet herself accidentally as a 10 year old). It may stem from a current life experience (I was hit by a reversing van, rendering me concussed and unconscious, so I am very nervous around vans now).

We may have learned to be anxious because we had an anxious parent and this becomes a blueprint for our way of thinking. We can become anxious through ingesting certain substances (any mind altering substances, legal or illegal, including some medication) or we may become ill, either physically or mentally, and anxiety can be one of the symptoms. Anxiety can manifest itself in panic attacks, phobias, PTSD (post-traumatic stress disorder), generalised anxiety disorder or OCD.

While there are some medications for reducing anxiety, it is important to note that finding the cause will go a long way towards either eliminating it or reducing the impact on daily life. CBT therapy has been found to be very effective as it challenges our irrational thoughts and beliefs and can also help us to change our behaviours as well as the way we think. The therapist will address issues such as catastrophizing, all or nothing thinking, 'shoulds and oughts', and similar thinking errors.

More severe cases of anxiety where the person has been exposed to very traumatic events sometimes benefit from a treatment called EMDR (Eye Movement Desensitisation and Reprocessing). Some phobias respond well to hypnotherapy (e.g. fear of flying, spiders, vomiting, to name but a few).

It is important to remember though that a small amount of anxiety serves the purpose of making us vigilant and aware of our surroundings, keeping us safe and alive. It is a protective mechanism that can sometimes activate the fight or flight response, a reaction dating back to the Stone Age. You either run, or get eaten as prey. So when our flight response is activated the heart beats faster, we may sweat excessively, feel nauseous and dizzy, hyperventilate, and have other physical symptoms. All these are so that the body can rid itself of anything it does not need, to make running more effective. People often experience this as a panic attack where anxiety activates all systems to get ready to run.

Printed in Great Britain
by Amazon

13845987R00067

CW00519282

Deadly Women
Volume Two

18 Shocking
True Murder Cases

Robert Keller

Please Leave Your Review of This Book At
http://bit.ly/kellerbooks

ISBN-13: 978-1979643450

ISBN-10: 1979643458

© 2017 by Robert Keller

robertkellerauthor.com

Table of Contents

Laurie Bembenek

In the early hours of May 28, 1981, someone entered the Milwaukee, Wisconsin home that Christine Schultz shared with her sons Sean, 10, and Shannon, 8. Moving silently and sure-footed through the darkened residence, the intruder worked his way up the stairs and peeked into the room where the boys lay sleeping. After a moment, he walked over to Sean's bed and placed a hand over the youngster's mouth. When the boy's eyes flew open, the stranger shushed him by raising a finger to his lips. "You stay here," he growled. "Don't leave your room." Then, like a phantom, he tiptoed across the carpeted floor and into the hallway. In that brief glimpse, Sean took in two important details about the man. He had long, reddish hair, drawn into a ponytail. And he wore black shoes similar to the ones favored by Sean's father, a Milwaukee police officer.

Sean, terrified by the brief encounter, was momentarily uncertain what to do. The stranger had headed down the hall toward his mother's bedroom. Steeling himself, the boy swung his legs out of bed and crept across the room to wake his brother.

The intruder, meanwhile, had entered the master bedroom where Christine Schultz lay sleeping. Shaking the woman roughly awake, he shoved a short-barreled .38 revolver into her face and told her to be quiet if she wanted her sons to live. Then he produced a length of plastic-coated clothesline and tied her hands in front of her, leaving her lying on her side, facing him. Christine had done everything she'd been asked and had put up no resistance. That, apparently, was not enough to appease the attacker. He shifted the gun and placed it directly against her chest. In the bedroom down the hall, the boys heard their mother cry out, "Oh God, no, please don't do that!" Then came the ugly, flat report of the revolver. The boys raced out into the hallway, just in time to see the stranger emerge from their mother's room, stuffing something into his pocket as he walked. Without saying a word, he hustled past them and down the stairs. Moments later, they heard the front door slam.

It was Sean who phoned for help, placing a call to his mother's boyfriend, Stewart Honeck, a Milwaukee police officer. Honeck immediately called for backup and then headed for Christine's house, getting there just as two police cruisers screeched to a halt outside. Honeck was the first to see Christine, noting right away that she wasn't breathing. She was lying on her right side, her hands bound in front of her with a clothesline-type cord, a blue bandanna wrapped around her head, her yellow t-shirt bearing a ragged, blood-encrusted bullet hole. An autopsy would later reveal that she'd been killed by a single .38 slug that had entered just below the shoulder and followed a downward trajectory towards the heart. The muzzle of the weapon had been in contact with her chest when it was fired.

Even before those details emerged, the police had uncovered some intriguing clues at the crime scene. They had a description of the suspect, who the boys described as a tall man wearing a green running suit and a military-style fatigue jacket. The man had worn a ski mask, but he had long reddish hair, worn in a ponytail, that trailed out of the back of the mask. He'd also worn "police shoes," according to Sean. The kind that his father wore, the kind that all Milwaukee cops wore. That piece of evidence left detectives in a potentially difficult situation. Were they investigating one of their own?

The obvious suspects were Christine's ex-husband, Elfred "Fred" Schultz, and her current boyfriend, Stewart Honeck, both of who were cops. The two men had once been friends, but Honeck's relationship with Christine had driven a wedge between them. The Schultzes divorce had been acrimonious and Fred Schultz resented his wife entertaining her new lover in the house that he had built. Was that, maybe, the motive? Perhaps, but Fred Schultz had a cast-iron alibi. At the time of the murder, he'd been investigating a burglary in another part of town. His partner backed him up.

What then of Stewart Honeck? According to his account of events, he'd had dinner at Christine's and had then sat watching TV for a while after Christine put the boys to bed. Christine had driven him home at around 11:30 and later they'd spent some time talking on the phone. Then, he'd gone to bed. It did not amount to an alibi as such, but Honeck also did not have a motive. He was, by all accounts, in love with Christine and had recently asked her to marry him.

So if neither of the men in Christine's life was the killer, then who was? While canvassing the neighborhood, detectives heard of a local weirdo named Gil Mende, who was often seen wearing a green running suit like that worn by the killer and who was apparently obsessed with Christine. Mende was questioned but never considered a serious suspect. The investigation appeared to have stalled.

Then came a startling turn of events. It emerged that Fred Schultz had lied about his alibi. The burglary that he and his partner had supposedly investigated on the night of the shooting had actually been picked up by another team of detectives.

Not wanting to alert Schultz to this latest piece of intelligence, investigators brought in his partner. Under questioning, the man quickly cracked and admitted that the alibi had been a lie. However, he insisted that it had not been intended to cover up a murder, but rather the fact that he and Schultz had been drinking in a downtown Milwaukee bar while on duty. That story checked out – sort of. Staff at the bar could recall Schultz being there but no one could recall what time he left. It was time to bring Fred Schultz in for questioning.

Interrogating a fellow detective is always difficult for investigators, much like a magician trying to outfox a fellow illusionist with a trick. None of the usual tactics are likely to work. The investigators, therefore, got straight down to it, asking Schultz outright if he'd killed his ex-wife. Schultz insisted that he hadn't and offered to take a polygraph. The investigators were happy to take him up on that offer.

The results of that session, as it turned out, would veer the case in an entirely different direction. Shultz passed every question put to him with flying colors, all except one, the question of whether anyone but he had access to his gun safe. He answered "No," sending the needle off the charts. Following up on that piece of information, detectives obtained a warrant for his personal revolver and test fired it. The results confirmed that this was the weapon that had killed Christine Schultz. And as Fred Schultz apparently had an alibi, that left just one possible suspect, his new wife Laurie.

Lawrencia "Laurie" Bembenek was an interesting woman. Beautiful and intelligent, she was the daughter of a police officer and had once served on the force herself. However, this was in an era when female officers were generally frowned upon, and Laurie soon found herself at odds with her fellow officers and also with the hierarchy. Unlike other female cops, Laurie was not prepared to keep her head below the precipice and simply ignore the barrage of discriminatory behavior directed at her on a daily basis. She took a stand, reporting the abuse and also other incidents of corruption she uncovered. Evidence was passed to the authorities showing cops selling drugs and pornography, cops taking money and sex in exchange for favors. None of these revelations resulted in action being taken. Instead, the machine turned on Bembenek herself. After her former roommate, Judy Zess, reported that she and Laurie had smoked a joint together at a rock concert, Bembenek was given a choice, hand in her badge or face an inquiry and possible dismissal. Disgusted, she resigned from the force.

After quitting the Milwaukee PD, Bembenek worked for a brief time as a waitress at a Lake Geneva Playboy Club. It was there that she acquired the nickname "Bambi" which would later be widely used by the press (and which she reportedly hated). She later found work as a security guard at Marquette University. It was

while working there that she met Fred Schultz, fresh from his
acrimonious divorce and eager to get back in the saddle. He
aggressively pursued Laurie for three months before she agreed to
be his wife. They were married on January 30, 1981.

What Laurie didn't realize, perhaps, was the baggage that her
marriage to Fred entailed. His divorce from Christine had been
extremely bitter, with Fred having to hand over the family home,
as well as $700 a month in child support. Laurie, according to
some accounts, resented Fred having to part with this money. One
witness even came forward to suggest that she'd been trying to
recruit a hitman to kill Christine. To the cops, this sounded like
motive. And as Bembenek also had access to the murder weapon
and to the Schultz residence (her husband, Fred, still had a set of
keys), she was elevated to the top of the suspect list. The final
piece of evidence was the discovery of a reddish-brown wig in the
plumbing system at Bembenek's apartment building.

Laurie Bembenek was taken into custody on June 24, 1981, and
despite her vociferous protestations of innocence, she was
charged with the murder of Christine Schultz. Her trial, in March
1982, would last for three weeks, with the judge noting in his
summation that he'd never come across a prosecution that relied
so strongly on circumstantial evidence. That observation
notwithstanding, Laurie Bembenek was found guilty of first-
degree murder. She was sentenced to life in prison at Wisconsin's
Taycheedah Correctional Institution. There were three separate
appeals, all of which Bembenek lost.

There are many reasons to believe that Laurie Bembenek got a bad
rap - two sets of unidentified fingerprints found at the crime scene,

for example, were never identified; Christine Schultz had blood under her fingernails, suggesting that she'd scratched her killer, yet Bembenek had no visible scratches in the days after the crime; the wig shop owner, who'd testified that Bembenek had purchased a reddish wig from her shop, paying by check, was proven to be wrong; Bembenek did not even have a checking account.

In addition, there were weaknesses in the prosecution case which the defense should have seized on but failed to do. The "expert" called to give evidence on hairs found on the victim was not an expert at all but had only six weeks training in forensics; blood found at the scene was not examined; neither were Bembenek's police-issue shoes, as supposedly worn by the killer; Frederick Horenburger, a convicted felon whose M.O. exactly matched the Schultz killing and who had bragged in prison that he'd committed the crime, was never presented as an alternate suspect; Bembenek's former friend, Judy Zess, was later proven to have committed perjury on the stand.

None of this made any difference to Laurie Bembenek. She was locked up for life, and although the prospect of parole hadn't been ruled out, she was likely to be a very old woman before she ever walked free. Then, ten years into her sentence, an opportunity opened up and Bembenek took it, escaping through an unbarred laundry window on July 15, 1990. With the help of Nick Gugliatto, who she'd met while he was visiting another prisoner, she fled to Thunder Bay, Ontario.

Many people in Milwaukee believed that Bembenek had gotten a raw deal and supported her escape. It was common, at that time, to see bumper stickers with the slogan "Run, Bambi, Run," and there were even rallies held in support of her. However, Bambi's freedom would be short-lived. Three months after her escape, she was spotted by an American tourist who reported her to the Canadian authorities. Despite a plea for refugee status (on the basis that she was being persecuted by the police department and judicial system of Wisconsin), she was returned to the United States.

Bembenek's flight had, however, achieved one thing. It had forced an inquiry into the original police investigation. Seven major blunders were highlighted, any one of which might have negated the decision to charge Bembenek with murder. Rather than risk a retrial, the state offered a deal, allowing Bembenek to plead "no contest" to a charge of second-degree murder in return for a reduced sentence, amounting to time served. Bembenek accepted and walked free.

The case of Bambi Bembenek has become one of the most widely covered in American history, spawning a couple of movies, a TV mini-series, and several books. Laurie Bembenek herself was to become somewhat of a celebrity. After her release, she graduated from the University of Wisconsin-Parkside with an honors degree in Humanities; she wrote a book about her case called "Woman on Trial" and did a book tour which included an appearance on Oprah; she became a sought-after speaker and an artist who showed her paintings at a number of galleries.

But as the case faded from public awareness, so too did the invitations and the galas, and eventually Laurie fell on hard times. She began living with a drug dealer and was arrested on possession charges, spending two weeks in prison. Then she contracted Hepatitis C. Eventually, she moved to Washington State where, almost penniless, she tried to start a new life.

Bambi Bembenek died of liver failure at a hospice facility in Portland, Oregon, on November 20, 2010. She was 52 years old.

Kristen Gilbert

Kristen Gilbert was born Kristen Strickland on November 13, 1967. When she was six months old, her family relocated to Fall River, Massachusetts, where Kristen would later be enrolled in kindergarten. She was a happy, lively child, although her demeanor changed somewhat after the birth of her younger sister. Kristen, seven years old at the time, seemed to resent the attention given to her sibling. She responded by inventing ailments and illnesses and by telling tall tales. One of her favorites was that she was related to Lizzie Borden, the infamous axe murderess who had lived in Fall River.

This almost obsessive need for attention only seemed to deepen as Kristen grew older. Although popular with boys, she seldom maintained a relationship for very long, due to her neurotic, overly possessive behavior. When a relationship inevitably broke down, she'd become abusive. More than one former boyfriend found his home or car vandalized. Some even reported threats of physical violence.

These negative traits notwithstanding, Kristen was an intelligent girl who graduated high school at age sixteen and thereafter enrolled on a nursing course at Greenfield Community College. In 1988, she gained certification as a registered nurse. Later that year, she married Glenn Gilbert and, in 1989, she gained a position on the staff of the Veterans Hospital at Northampton, Massachusetts. An avid reader on medical matters, Kristen was an excellent and knowledgeable nurse. She was also pretty and photogenic, leading to her being featured on the cover of "VA Practitioner" magazine in April 1990.

Yet despite this stellar beginning to her nursing career, not all was well in the life of Kristen Gilbert. There were problems in her marriage harking right back to the honeymoon when she'd threatened her husband with a knife during an argument. Glenn Gilbert had quickly learned that his wife was far from stable. She veered between elation and depression, threatened suicide on numerous occasions, and spent recklessly. She was also somewhat of a hypochondriac, a condition that seemed to intensify after the birth of her son in 1990.

And things at work were hardly much better. 1990 saw the beginning of a worrying pattern of patient deaths while Gilbert was on duty. No one suspected anything untoward, but the other nurses began to refer jokingly to Gilbert as the "Angel of Death."

Not everyone saw the humor in the situation, though. One alert clerical worker noticed that the death rate on the ward was three times higher when Gilbert was on duty. She reported her concerns to her superiors but was told not to make unfounded aspersions.

In November 1993, Kristen gave birth to a second son. By then, her marriage to Glenn Gilbert was already in deep trouble and she was telling her work colleagues that she was thinking about a divorce. She had, in any case, cast her eye elsewhere, to a handsome hospital security guard named James Perrault. She began making a concerted effort to lose weight and started flirting openly with Perrault. It wasn't long before they were sneaking off to the parking lot to have sex in his car.

Shortly after Kristen began her affair with James Perrault, her husband Glenn became seriously ill. He was taken to the hospital where tests found extremely low potassium levels, a condition almost unheard of in a man of his age. It would later be speculated that Kristen had been feeding him drugs to suppress the mineral and thus elevate his blood pressure to dangerously high levels. A short while after Glenn was hospitalized, the couple split, with Kristen moving into her own apartment, leaving the children in Glenn's care.

Meanwhile, at the VA hospital, Kristen Gilbert's patients continued to die. On August 21, 1995, Gilbert was seen entering a ward holding a syringe. A short while later, Korean War veteran Stanley Jagodowski began shouting for a nurse, complaining that his arm hurt. Within minutes, he went into cardiac arrest. Despite the best efforts of medics, he died later that day. Over the months that followed, several other patients died in startlingly similar circumstances, all of them while Kristen Gilbert was on duty.

And yet, amazingly, hospital administrators failed to see anything unusual. It was only after three of Gilbert's colleagues raised concerns about the number of cardiac arrest deaths on the ward, that management agreed to take action. A subsequent inquiry noted that vials of epinephrine, a drug that mimics the effects of adrenaline, were missing. It was then that hospital managers called in the police.

The inquiry was far-reaching and included the exhumation of four patients, all of who were found to have high levels of epinephrine in their bodies. After supplies of the drug were found stashed at Gilbert's house, she was placed under arrest and charged with killing three patients - Henry Hudon, 35, Kenneth Cutting, 41, and Edward Skwira, 69 - and attempting to kill two more. A fourth murder, that of Stanley Jagodowski, was later added to the rap sheet. Evidence suggested that Gilbert had injected her victims with epinephrine, causing their hearts to race out of control and eventually fail.

Why exactly Gilbert murdered her patients is unclear, although psychiatrists suggested that she was suffering from Munchausen by Proxy syndrome and wanted to draw attention to herself and her ability to deal with emergency situations. Specifically, they believe that she was trying to impress her lover, James Perrault. VA hospital rules mandate that hospital police must be present at any medical emergency, so Perrault was often in attendance.

And there were many emergency situations when Kristen Gilbert was on duty. Most of the patients survived, but of the 63 that didn't, 37 died under Kristen Gilbert's care. And that number may be only the tip of the iceberg. Investigators believe that Gilbert may have been responsible for as many as 80 deaths.

Kristen Gilbert was eventually convicted in federal court on March 14, 2001. Although Massachusetts does not have capital punishment, Gilbert was eligible for the death penalty, as her crimes had been committed on federal property.

However, a sentence of death requires a unanimous verdict on the part of the jury and, as that was not achieved, the judgment defaulted automatically to life in prison without the possibility of parole. An additional 20 years was added for the attempted murder convictions.

Kristen Gilbert is currently incarcerated at a federal prison in Texas.

Ruth Ellis

Ruth Neilson was born in the town of Rhyl, on the northeast coast of Wales, on October 9, 1926, the third of six children. Her mother was a Belgian refugee, her father a musician who was often away, plying his trade on Atlantic cruise ships. During her childhood, the family moved to Basingstoke, and later to London. By then, Ruth had grown into a precocious 14-year-old, who had already quit school and was working as a waitress. It was while thus employed that the 17-year-old Ruth became pregnant by a married Canadian soldier in 1944. Her son, Clare Andrea Neilson (known to the family as Andy) was born the next year, although Ruth played very little part in his upbringing, those duties falling mainly to the boy's grandmother.

Ruth Neilson, in truth, was never cut out for the role of a stay-at-home mom. She had by now adopted a whole new persona. Petite and pretty, and with hair dyed platinum blonde, she was a nightclub hostess with a sideline in nude modelling. She was also a part-time prostitute and, in 1950, she became pregnant by one of her regular customers. Unwilling to take on the responsibility of another child, she had an illegal abortion, terminating the pregnancy in its third month.

In November 1950, Ruth accepted a marriage proposal from one of the regulars at the hostess club where she worked. George Ellis was 16 years her senior, a heavy drinker with a violent temper and an extremely possessive nature. Unsurprisingly, he and Ruth clashed frequently, and when she fell pregnant, he denied paternity, resulting in the marriage breaking down. Ruth's daughter, Georgina, was born in 1951. With no financial support from the child's father, Ruth was forced to move back in with her parents and to return to work as a nightclub hostess. It was two years later, in 1953, that she met David Blakely, and the seeds of disaster, for both of their lives, were sown.

Ruth was at the time managing a drinking establishment called the Little Club, where Blakely was a regular. He was handsome and well-educated, a "toff" in the parlance of the day. But he was also a womanizer and a heavy drinker. At the time he met Ruth, he was, in fact, engaged to another woman. Still, the attraction between them was instant and mutual, and it wasn't long before Blakely had moved into Ruth's apartment above the club. It was only then that she began to see the dark side of her new paramour. The two of them fought regularly, with Blakely was not afraid to use his fists on the five-foot-two Ruth to settle a dispute. The relationship was extremely volatile, with Blakely moving in and out of the apartment several times. In the wake of all of this turbulence, Ruth became pregnant again. Again she underwent an abortion. And perhaps seeking some stability among all of this discord, she took on a new lover.

Desmond Cussens was considerably more staid than David Blakely. During the war, he'd served as an RAF pilot. Now, he was the director of a family business, a retail tobacconist with outlets in London and Wales. It wasn't long before Ruth had moved into his luxury apartment near Oxford Street and become his mistress.

But for all of his faults, David Blakely remained Ruth's one true love. The two continued to see one another, meeting up for trysts in hotel rooms and at friends' homes. Blakely, however, was jealous of her relationship with Cussens, and Ruth was equally embittered by the stories she heard of his many conquests. If the relationship had been volatile before, it reached a whole new level now, with confrontations often becoming violent.

In late 1955, Blakely proposed that the only way for them to resolve their problems was for both of them to end their philandering and to settle down to married life together. Ruth gleefully accepted, but a month later, another fight broke out when Ruth told Blakely that she was pregnant. He, unsurprisingly, raised questions about the child's paternity. Ruth reacted furiously and in the ensuing scuffle, Blakely punched her in the stomach, causing her to miscarry. Thereafter, he refused to see her, leading to her becoming increasingly frantic. She thought that she might have lost him this time for good. And that was a scenario that Ruth Ellis was not prepared to countenance.

Matters eventually came to a head on Easter Sunday, April 10, 1955. Blakely had been staying at the home of friends, Anthony and Carole Findlater, and word had reached Ruth that he was having an affair with the family's newly employed nanny. Intent on confronting him about the allegations, Ruth hailed a taxi in Oxford

Street at around 9 a.m. that morning, directing the cabbie to the Findlater's home at 29 Tanza Road, Hampstead. In her coat pocket, she was carrying a .38 revolver, the property of her live-in lover, Desmond Cussens.

Ruth had just arrived at Tanza Road, when she saw Blakely get into his car and drive off. She instructed the cabbie to follow, which he did, tracking Blakely to the Magdala public house in South Hill Park, Hampstead. After exiting the cab, Ruth waited in the doorway of Henshaw's news agents, determined to confront Blakely the minute he emerged. She did not have long to wait.

Just after 9:30, David Blakely walked out of the pub with his friend, Clive Gunnell. As he passed, Ruth stepped into his path and said, "Hello, David." Blakely, however, paid her no heed, instead skirting around her and walking to his car. "David!" Ruth shouted after him, but still he ignored her. He was digging in his pocket for his car keys when Ruth drew the revolver and fired.

The first shot was wild and it missed. The second, fired as Blakely turned and ran, did not. It struck him in the back and he collapsed to the pavement, mortally wounded. That, however, was not enough for Ellis. She stood over the helpless man and pumped three more bullets into him, the last fired at such close range that it left powder burns on his skin. A final shot missed its target but ricocheted up and hit a passerby, Gladys Yule, in the hand. Ellis, in an apparent state of shock, now turned to Clive Gunnell, cowering behind a car, "Will you call the police, Clive?" she said.

That request, as it turned out, was unnecessary. An off-duty police officer, Alan Thompson, had heard the shots and come running. He immediately disarmed the dazed Ruth, shoving the still-smoking revolver into his coat pocket. "I am guilty. I'm a little confused," Ruth said as he disarmed her.

Ruth Ellis was taken to Hampstead police station where she gave a detailed confession and was charged with murder. Blakely's body, meanwhile, had been taken to a nearby hospital where he was declared dead on arrival. He'd suffered multiple bullet wounds which had perforated his intestines, liver, lung, aorta, and windpipe.

The murder trial of Ruth Ellis began at Court Number One of the Old Bailey on Monday, June 20, 1955, before Mr. Justice Havers. Ruth's solicitor had asked her to tone down her appearance but she had ignored him. She seemed determined to look her best for her big moment. Her hair was freshly coiffured and bleached to its customary platinum blonde, and she was dressed stylishly in a black suit and white silk blouse.

Whether or not this made an impression on the jury, one way or the other, we will never know. In the end, it was Ruth's own testimony that would lead to her conviction. Asked by the prosecutor, Mr. Christmas Humphreys, what her intention was when she fired at Blakely, Ruth replied truthfully: "It's obvious when I shot him I intended to kill him."

And with that, she all but sealed her fate. Her reply gave the jury no leeway at all. They returned a guilty verdict after just 14 minutes of deliberation. Under the law, that verdict carried a mandatory death sentence. Ellis accepted the judge's ruling without emotion. "Thank you," she said after the sentence was read. Then she turned and smiled at her friends seated in the public gallery before walking calmly down the stairs at the back of the dock. She was taken from there to Holloway and housed in the Condemned Unit, where she was placed on suicide watch, guarded round the clock by two female warders.

In the immediate aftermath of the trial, Ellis advised her attorneys that she did not wish to lodge an appeal. Her fate now rested in the hands of the Home Secretary, Gwilym Lloyd George, and he seemed disinclined to consider clemency, despite considerable pressure from the press and public and a recommendation from the trial judge that he should commute the sentence. On Monday, July 11, he announced his decision. Ruth Ellis was to hang.

Justice moved swiftly in those days. Prisoner 9656 Ruth Ellis would spend just three weeks and two days in the condemned cell before her execution date came around on July 13, 1955. On the Tuesday evening, the eve of the hanging, the Governor at Holloway had to call in police reinforcements when a raucous crowd gathered outside the prison gates and began chanting and singing Ruth's name.

Within the walls, meanwhile, preparations were continuing apace for the execution.

Ruth was weighed and the correct length of drop calculated; the gallows were tested using a sand bag weighing 103 pounds, the same weight as the condemned. At around 7.00 a.m. on the morning of the execution, the trap was reset and the rope left dangling, with the noose at around chest height. A cross was placed on the far wall of the execution chamber at Ruth's request.

In the death cell, meanwhile, Ruth wrote a letter to Blakely's mother begging forgiveness for causing his death and declaring that she still loved him and always would. She was visited in her cell by the Catholic Bishop of Stepney and by the prison doctor, who gave her a large brandy to steady her nerves. Finally, she was fitted with the canvas knickers which were compulsory for all female prisoners undergoing execution.

At nine o'clock precisely, the executioner, Albert Pierrepoint, entered the cell and pinioned Ruth's hands behind her back with a leather strap. He then led her the 15 feet from the death cell to the gallows. Pierrepoint, who for years after kept up a correspondence with Ruth's sister Muriel, later commented that she went bravely to her death and uttered not a word during the entire process. Twelve seconds after being led from her cell, Ruth Ellis plummeted through the trap door to oblivion.

But although her execution was completed with the minimum of fuss and without ruction, its aftermath would be anything but quiet. The hanging triggered widespread condemnation, with newspapers and political appointees inundated with letters from disgusted citizens. Those waves would continue to grow over the next decade, leading to the eventual abolishment of capital punishment in Great Britain in 1965.

Ruth's death also had a profound impact on her family. In 1969, her mother, Berta Neilson, attempted suicide by gassing herself in her apartment. Although she was saved by a family member, she never fully recovered and remained an invalid for the rest of her life. Ruth's son, Andy, who was 10 at the time of his mother's execution, also found it difficult to come to terms with her death. He endured lifelong psychological issues, eventually committing suicide in 1982. Ruth's former husband, George Ellis, also killed himself, leaving their daughter, Georgina, an orphan. Georgina was later adopted. She died of cancer at the age of 50.

Ruth Ellis was originally buried within the walls of Holloway prison but was later disinterred and laid to rest in a churchyard in Buckinghamshire. The prosecutor at her trial, Mr. Christmas Humphreys, paid the cost of the funeral.

Sylvia Seegrist

Long before the shooting started on that fateful day in October 1985, everyone knew that there was something seriously wrong with Sylvia Seegrist. The 25-year-old Pennsylvania native had a long history of erratic behavior and had been in and out of mental facilities since her mid-teens. She'd been diagnosed as a paranoid schizophrenic and, in her case, the sickness manifested itself in a deep-seated hatred towards all humanity. She was perpetually angry, constantly raging against the injustices of the world. "When I heard about the shooting at the mall," one man later testified, "I knew immediately that it was her."

The shooting that this man was referring to occurred at around 4 p.m. on Wednesday, October 30, 1985. The Springfield Mall, just outside of Philadelphia, was busy that day, with many shoppers stocking up on Halloween goodies. In fact when the first shots were fired, most of those who heard them thought that it was some kind of Halloween prank.

It wasn't. Just moments earlier Sylvia Seegrist had rolled into the mall's parking lot in her white Datsun B-210. She was dressed in olive green military fatigues, a knit cap and shiny black boots. When she got out of the car she was holding a .22-caliber semi-automatic Ruger rifle.

Seegrist started shooting almost immediately, firing off two shots which fortunately missed a pedestrian. As the man ducked behind a vehicle, Seegrist strode purposefully towards the mall entrance where she encountered a woman drawing cash from an ATM. The bullet fired in the woman's direction failed to find its target, and Seegrist then turned and shot at a man just as he entered the mall. That shot also missed, but the next one tragically did not. Two-year-old Recife Cosmen was standing outside the Magic Pan restaurant when a bullet tore through his chest and killed him instantly. His cousins, Tiffany Wootson, 10, and Kareen Wootson, 9, were also hit but would recover from facial and chest wounds. Barely pausing to examine the carnage she'd wrought, Seegrist walked on, entering the mall proper.

By now shoppers had realized that this was no Halloween prank. This was some psycho with a gun, someone intent on murder. They scattered, screaming, as they dashed into nearby shops and sought cover. The shooter, meanwhile, continued on, firing at any target in her path. Bullets shattered the plate glass window at an Oriental rug store; a hail of gunfire raked the ceiling of the Rite Aid drugstore, causing staff and customers to dive for cover. It was a miracle that no one was hit. At a Kinney shoe store, Seegrist fired again, pumping three rounds into 64-year-old Augusto Ferrara and killing him. Then she walked on, muttering angrily to herself, lifting her rifle whenever a target appeared. Several more people were shot and slumped to the ground, their blood stark against the muted tile of the mall walkways. A woman was screaming, begging someone to help her injured husband, but no one came to her assistance. No one was brave enough to break cover and face down the shooter.

The rampage had now been going on for just three minutes, but already the toll was two dead and eight wounded. A young girl had been shot twice in the stomach and lay groaning on the ground, a woman had taken a bullet in the back and was being attended by her friend. Nearby a teenaged girl stood dazed and clutched her injured wrist which was seeping blood.

John Laufer, a 24-year-old graduate student, had come to the mall that day with his girlfriend. Like the other patrons he had heard the shooting and had assumed at first that it was a prank. He hadn't yet seen the blood on the ground or the dead and wounded when he spotted a woman walking towards him. She was dressed in army fatigues and carrying a rifle.

This, Laufer assumed, was the perpetrator of the shooting prank and it made him angry. Didn't she know how foolhardy her actions were, firing blanks in a crowded space? She might spark a stampede; people might get hurt. Walking towards the woman, Laufer barely flinched when she lifted her weapon and pointed it at him. Why would he when he believed that the rifle was loaded with blanks? "Cut that out," he demanded as he reached the woman, grabbed her arm and twisted it behind her back. He then yanked the rifle from her grasp. "I'm a woman," she mumbled, "and I have family problems, and I have seizures."

Laufer didn't bother responding. He unceremoniously marched his captive into a nearby shoe store and sat her down in a chair. Then

he instructed her to stay there while he went in search of a mall
security guard. Amazingly Seegrist complied. She was sitting
meekly in the same spot when Laufer returned with the guard.
Moments later she was in cuffs.

In the meantime, the local 911 line had been bombarded with calls
from panicked mall shoppers; emergency responders had been
dispatched and were racing towards the scene. The shooting had
lasted less than four minutes during which Seegrist had fired 20
rounds. Two people were dead and eight wounded. One of those
victims, 67-year-old Ernest Trout, would die later in hospital.
Seegrist still had ten rounds left in her magazine when John Laufer
brought her killing spree to an end.

The shooting rampage at Springfield Mall was far from the most
lethal in American history. But it was unique in that the shooter
was a woman. Sylvia Seegrist was catapulted suddenly into the
spotlight, a figure of national infamy. What the nation most wanted
to know was: Who was this woman and what had possessed her to
commit such an atrocity?

Sylvia Wynanda Seegrist was born on July 31, 1960, in
Pennsylvania. The early part of her life was by all accounts entirely
normal. Sylvia was a bright and happy child until the age of 13,
when according to her mother she was sexually assaulted by her
grandfather. After that her behavior went into a steep downward
spiral, and by 15 she was smoking pot and having sex with
neighborhood boys. Then things got even worse and she began
displaying signs of mental illness, resulting in her removal from
school and committal to a psychiatric hospital where she was
diagnosed with paranoid schizophrenia. That triggered a 10-year

cycle of violent episodes punctuated by committal to various mental institutions. But Sylvia was always released once her behavior stabilized. Then she'd refuse to take her medication and the sequence would begin all over again. It culminated eventually in that horrific day at the Springfield Mall.

And yet no one can say that there weren't warning signs. Seegrist lived within walking distance of the mall and visited it often. There she'd stalk the halls in her army fatigues, going in and out of the stores and harassing customers and staff. The manager of the drugstore where she picked up her meds even came up with a nickname for her. He called her "Ms. Rambo." Sylvia also once showed up at a local health club and did a full workout in her military uniform before spending an hour sitting fully clothed in the spa. Another popular hangout was the library where she would take out a book (usually something military related) and spend an entire afternoon muttering to herself while she tried to translate it into Russian using a Russian/English dictionary.

And her behavior at home was equally bizarre. She would spend hours at night marching up and down the stairs in her military garb. On other occasions, she was observed raking leaves in the chilly pre-dawn hours. Other behaviors were more frightening. She'd sometimes accost neighbors in the corridor, shrieking curses and ranting about the coming nuclear war or how the entire world was against her. And at times, her anger bubbled over into actual violence. Once she was arrested for trying to strangle her mother on a busy city street. Another time she plunged a pair of scissors into the back of a mental health worker.

It seems astounding that a woman who was so obviously disturbed should be allowed to purchase a semi-automatic rifle. But Sylvia Seegrist was able to do just that, acquiring a Ruger .22-caliber from the sporting goods counter at Best Products. Seegrist had stated on a form that she had no history of mental illness, and the store was not required to check. She paid $107 and walked away with a lethal weapon. That was toward the end of September. Thereafter Seegrist joined a rifle club and spent a month honing her marksmanship. Those skills had been put to deadly effect on October 30.

As a diagnosed schizophrenic and someone who displayed clear signs of mental illness, most observers were of the opinion that Seegrist would be declared unfit to stand trial. However, the State of Pennsylvania was determined to bring the matter before a jury, and after several experts agreed that there was clear evidence of pre-planning, it was decided the Seegrist would have to answer for her acts.

So it was that on June 18, 1986, seven months after the shootings, Sylvia Seegrist stood before a judge charged with three counts of murder and seven counts of attempted murder and assault.

Over the next eight days, a battle was fought, one side focusing on the events on October 30, the other on Sylvia Seegrist's long history of mental illness. Eventually it was left to the twelve jurors to decide, and the judge offered them four possible outcomes. They could find Seegrist guilty, not guilty, guilty but mentally ill, or not guilty by reason of insanity.

After nine hours of deliberation, the jury delivered its verdict, finding Seegrist guilty but mentally ill. That judgment, of course, meant that Seegrist would do prison time, and the sentence of the court reflected the seriousness of the crimes – three consecutive life sentences for the murders, ten years for each of the seven victims who she had wounded. Seegrist, who had expressed a preference for the electric chair, seemed disappointed at the outcome.

Sylvia Seegrist was sent to serve out her prison term at the State Correctional Institution at Muncy, Pennsylvania. There, with the help of anti-psychotic medications, her condition stabilized to the extent that she was able to complete a college degree. She ended up tutoring fellow inmates in mathematics. She was also able to come to terms with the impact of her shooting spree and to express remorse for what she had done.

Whether that remorse is genuine or an attempt to gain parole, we do not know. Seegrist has readily admitted that she hopes to be released one day. It is uncertain whether that wish will ever be granted.

Kathleen Folbigg

When Kathleen Folbigg was 18 months old, her father murdered her mother, dragging her out into the street and stabbing her 24 times in front of horrified neighbors. His motive, he later told police, was to save his daughter. "I had to kill her," he said, "because she would have killed my child."

Thomas John Britton was arrested that same day and would spend 14 years in prison. He would be deported to the United Kingdom following his release. For Kathleen, the results were almost as catastrophic. With no other relatives to care for her, she was made a ward of the state and placed in foster care.

In September 1970, the three-year-old Kathleen was fostered by a couple named Marlborough, who later expressed an interest in adopting her. Their motives were not entirely altruistic, as Deidre Marlborough treated the child as a virtual slave and prevented her making friends. Kathleen tolerated this treatment until she was 15. Then she quit school and started working at a series of low-paying jobs. At 20, she met and fell in love with Craig Folbigg, five years her senior. The couple settled in Mayfield, a suburb of Newcastle. Within a year, Kathleen was pregnant, and in February 1989, she delivered a healthy son who she named Caleb.

Five days after the birth, Kathleen took Caleb home, but a few days later she was back at the hospital, explaining to staff that the baby appeared to be having difficulty breathing. Doctors diagnosed a "lazy larynx," said it was nothing serious and assured her that Caleb would grow out of it. They were wrong.

At around 2:50 a.m. on February 19, 1989, Craig Folbigg woke to the sound of his wife screaming. He rushed to the sunroom where the baby slept and found Kathleen standing over the crib. "My baby," she wailed. "Something's wrong with my baby." Something certainly was wrong. Caleb Folbigg, just 20 days old, was dead. The official cause of death would be given as Sudden Infant Death Syndrome (SIDS) or "cot death."

Seven months on and Kathleen was pregnant again, delivering a son named Patrick in June 1990. Four months later, on October 19, Craig was again woken by his wife's screams. He rushed to the baby's room and again found Kathleen hovering over the baby. Lifting the child from the crib, Craig thought that he noted faint breathing. He immediately started mouth-to-mouth resuscitation and by the time the ambulance arrived had managed to revive Patrick.

The episode, however, had exacted a heavy toll on the tiny infant. He was blind, and doctors believed that he'd suffer epileptic fits for the rest of his life. As it turned out, the rest of his life was all too short.

On the morning of February 13, 1991, Kathleen phoned Craig at work, and in a frantic voice, told him: "It's happened again." Craig left work immediately and pulled up in front of his house just as the ambulance arrived. Patrick was rushed to hospital but was pronounced dead on arrival. An autopsy determined that the cause of death was an "acute asphyxiating event" resulting from an epileptic fit.

Devastated by the death of another child, the Folbiggs left Newcastle and moved to Thornton in March 1991. Eighteen months later, in October 1992, Kathleen gave birth to another child, a daughter this time, who the couple named Sarah. Sarah would survive for 11 months, longer than her siblings. But events soon picked up a familiar pattern: another late night crisis, another mad dash to the hospital, another baby dead. As in the case of Caleb, death was attributed to SIDS.

After Sarah's death, the Folbiggs moved again, this time settling in Hunter Valley, a popular wine-producing region north of Newcastle. Their fourth child, Laura, was born in August 1997 and remained healthy for the next 19 months. Then, at around midnight on March 1, 1999, Kathleen made an anxious call and summoned an ambulance. Emergency services staff arrived to find her performing CPR on her daughter. It was too late. The little girl was already dead.

But Laura was too old to have died from SIDS, so the coroner recorded her cause of death as "undetermined" and ordered a police investigation. It was the beginning of the end for Kathleen Folbigg.

Detective Sergeant Bernard Ryan was assigned to the case. And his suspicions were immediately aroused when he learned that four of the couple's children had died in similar circumstances. Still, his initial interviews with the Folbiggs turned up nothing untoward. Craig and Kathleen seemed genuinely distraught at the tragedies that had been visited upon them.

The Folbiggs' marriage, meanwhile, was breaking down, understandable perhaps under the circumstances. In March 2001, Kathleen moved out, leaving most of her personal possessions behind. It was while clearing out those possessions that Craig Folbigg made a horrific discovery. In a bedside drawer, he found Kathleen's diaries. The contents, he later told the court, made him "want to vomit." He took them immediately to the police.

Kathleen had been a keen diarist all her life and usually threw her journals away once they were full. These, however, she appeared to have overlooked. They told the story of a deeply disturbed woman. On the one hand, she wrote of her joy at becoming a mother. On the other, she spoke of the resentment she felt after each birth when the attention shifted away from her to the new baby. Tellingly, she spoke of how stress had "made her do terrible things" and how she had "flashes of rage, resentment and hatred" toward her children.

In another entry, written while she was pregnant with Laura, Folbigg alluded to previous actions that she regretted. "Obviously I'm my father's daughter. But I think losing my temper and being frustrated and everything has passed. I now just let things happen and go with the flow. An attitude I should of [sic] had with all my children. If given the chance, I'll have it with the next one."

Another, particularly chilling entry read: "With Sarah, all I wanted was for her to shut up. And one day, she did." It wasn't an admission of murder, but it was as close as the police could get to providing a motive.

Kathleen Folbigg was arrested at her home on April 19, 2001, and charged with murdering her four children. At her trial, the prosecution contended that she'd smothered each of the children because she could not deal with the day-to-day stresses of being a mother. Folbigg denied this, but the evidence against her was pretty damning. When the matter went to the jury, they took less than eight hours to find her guilty. The sentence of the court was forty years, with no possibility of parole for thirty. In 2005, this was reduced on appeal to thirty years, with no parole period for twenty-five.

Kathleen Folbigg is currently serving her time in protective isolation. Other prisoners take a very dim view of women who murder children, especially their own.

Mary Wilson

The groom was in his mid-seventies, the bride Mary Wilson was 66 and marrying for the third time. Still, no one could begrudge her a moment of happiness. After all, she'd been through a bleak time of late, losing two husbands and a live-in lover in the space of just two years. Not even her propensity for macabre humor could spoil the occasion. Asked about the amount of cake left over after the wedding party, Mrs. Wilson quipped "Oh, we'll just keep that for the funeral."

That remark turned out to be predictive. On the evening of November 12, 1957, Mary Wilson arrived at the home of a friend Grace Liddell in Hebburn-on-Tyne in Durham, northeast England. She said that her husband was feeling unwell and asked if she could spend the night. Mrs. Liddell, of course, consented.

The following morning, Grace Liddell agreed to accompany Mrs. Wilson back to her home in nearby Windy Nook. On arrival, Wilson handed Mrs. Liddell the front door key and insisted that she enter first. When she did, she was shocked to find Ernest

Wilson laid out on a table in the front room, quite obviously dead. A doctor was then called and ascertained that the retired engineer had expired several hours earlier. As he'd suffered from heart problems in his later years, it was assumed that he'd died of cardiac problems. That, at least, was what went on the death certificate.

So it was that just three weeks after taking her nuptials for a third time, Mary Wilson was widowed yet again. Nothing unusual in that, given the advanced ages of the men in question. But then rumors started to circulate. It began with another of Mary's off-color jokes. At her husband's funeral, she remarked to the undertaker that she should perhaps qualify for a group rate, given the amount of business she was sending his way. That quip eventually reached the ears of Detective Inspector Arthur Chapman who decided to look into it. His investigation would uncover the most unusual serial killer in British criminal history.

Mary Elizabeth Wilson was born at Hebburn, South Tyneside in 1893. Little is known about her early life, but we do know that, as a young woman, she began working as a servant to the Knowles family. While thus employed, she struck up a relationship with one of the family's sons, John Knowles, marrying him in 1912. They settled down to married life in Windy Nook, a suburb of Gateshead, Durham.

The marriage was by all accounts a contented one, if rather passionless. By the 1940s, husband and wife were still cohabitating although no longer sharing a bed. They had by now taken in a lodger, John Russell, and he and Mary soon became lovers. Mary's husband apparently knew about the relationship but was unperturbed by it. As long as his meals were cooked and his house kept clean, John Knowles was prepared to live and let live.

This cozy state of affairs continued for nearly a decade. Then in July 1955, Knowles suddenly fell ill with an unexplained ailment. Despite the best attention of his family doctor and the devoted nursing of his wife, he was dead within months. Apparently distraught at his passing, Mary moved home soon after, taking her lover with her.

All went well until Christmas 1955 when John Russell began showing symptoms that were remarkably similar to those of Mary's late husband. A doctor was called and attended to Russell, who appeared to be in severe pain. Mary, so recently widowed, hovered nearby, a phantom in black, clucking and fussing and occasionally dabbing at the tears that welled up in her eyes. When the doctor eventually departed, she swore to John Russell that she would be by his side no matter what. And Mary was good to her word. Over the weeks that followed, she attended diligently to her patient, preparing his meals and carrying up endless cups of tea from the kitchen. It was to no avail. Russell's condition deteriorated rapidly. By January 1956, he was dead.

Mary appears to have accepted the death of her lover stoically. She gave away his meager possessions to charity, cashed his small life insurance policy which named her as sole beneficiary and had his room repainted. Then she began casting about for a new companion, settling eventually on Oliver Leonard, a retired estate agent. Mary was by now 64 years old and well past her prime, but she was vivacious and outgoing and the elderly Leonard was soon

under her spell. They married in September 1956, less than nine
months after John Russell breathed his last.

But Mary soon regretted her hasty decision to remarry. Leonard
was set in his ways and so was she. They clashed frequently over
the most trivial of things. Barely a week into the marriage, she
decided that the situation needed to be redressed. Six days later, a
doctor was summoned to the Leonard household and found Oliver
Leonard dead. Mary, distraught and in tears, lamented to friends,
"I've been so terribly unlucky in love. It's almost as though I'm
blighted."

Oliver Leonard's death was attributed to a heart attack and his
widow benefitted by way of a £50 insurance policy and some
items of furniture. Over the weeks that followed, she appeared
suitably depressed, although her old spark soon returned and she
began casting about for a new companion. Thirteen months later,
she allowed herself to be wooed by retired engineer Ernest
Wilson. He lasted barely longer than Mary's previous spouse and
was ushered off to meet his maker after just two weeks of
matrimonial bliss. Now, however, Mary's ill-considered remarks
about surplus wedding cake and discounted funerals had reached
the ears of the authorities, and Detective Inspector Arthur
Chapman was determined to get to the bottom of the spate of
unexplained deaths.

Chapman began by trying to uncover a possible motive for
murder. But that avenue of investigation led him straight down a
cul-de-sac. Mary Wilson had received only paltry amounts on the
deaths of her husbands. The most handsome dividend was £100,
received from Ernest Wilson's estate. The smallest was just £20,

hardly a motive for wholesale slaughter. Still Chapman pushed on. Questioning neighbors turned up several examples of Mary's off-color wit and one other interesting anecdote. It appears that after the deaths of each of her husbands, Mary had started inquiring around the neighborhood after possible suitors, preferably elderly men with money and no family ties.

That, of course, did not amount to evidence of murder, but it was enough for Chapman to obtain exhumation orders on Oliver Leonard and Ernest Wilson. Chapman was present when the caskets were unearthed, and he was immediately struck by the absence of insect life in the soil. The reason was soon clear. Yellow phosphorus, a common ingredient in rat poison during that era, was found in the organs of each of the corpses. In short order, Mary Wilson found herself under arrest and charged with murder.

The "Merry Widow of Windy Nook," as the press was now dubbing her, made a most unlikely Black Widow. This was no femme fatale but a woman in her mid-sixties who looked even older. Whatever feminine allure she might once have possessed had long since deserted her. Still, Mary's neighbors were in no doubt that she was guilty of the charges levied against her, even if the accused murderess stoutly denied them.

The trial was swift and the verdict inevitable. Found guilty on two counts of murder (in the other two cases, autopsy results had been inconclusive due to the dissipation of the poison over time), Mary Elizabeth Wilson was sentenced to death by hanging. But Mary would never feel the rough fabric of the hangman's noose around her neck. Her sentence was commuted and she was sent to

Wandsworth Prison to serve out her life term. She died there on December 5, 1962, at the age of 70.

Diane Downs

At around 10:50 on the night of Thursday, May 19, 1983, a late-model red Nissan Pulsar with Arizona plates pulled up to the ER at McKenzie-Willamette Hospital in Springfield, Oregon. The driver, a blonde woman in her twenties, staggered from the vehicle. "Somebody just shot my kids!" she screamed, pointing back towards the car.

ER medics are, of course, used to dealing with such situations. Nurses Rose Martin and Shelby Day were out of the door in an instant, running towards the woman. Seeing that she was only slightly injured, they pointed her inside, then went to the aid of her passengers. Meanwhile, receptionist Judy Patterson, as is protocol in such cases, got on the phone to the police.

The first thing that nurses Martin and Day saw as they approached the car was blood, lots of it, sprayed across the interior, spattering the bodies of three small children. A blonde-haired girl was slumped in the passenger seat, another girl and a boy, no more than a toddler, in back. All appeared to have suffered gunshot wounds to their chests.

The children were pulled from the vehicle and rushed into the hospital where it was determined that one of them, the girl who had been in the front seat, was already dead. Meanwhile, with personnel from the ICU brought in to assist, a battle was waged to save the other two. Thanks to the skill of the medical professionals involved, 8-year-old Christie Downs and her 3-year-old brother, Danny, would eventually pull through. The dead girl was their sister, Cheryl, aged just 7.

Police officers from both Springfield and Lane Counties had in the interim responded to the call, and it was quickly determined that the crime fell within the jurisdiction of the Lane County Sheriff's Office. Sergeant Robin Rutherford then spoke to the children's mother. She said that her name was Diane Downs and that she'd been driving to her home in Springfield after visiting a friend in Marcola. As she'd turned onto Old Mohawk Road, a man had flagged her down. He'd demanded her keys. When she refused to hand them over, he leaned into the car and fired at her children.

Without waiting to get the finer details, Rutherford immediately put out an APB on the suspect. If there was a madman on the highway taking potshots at travelers, he needed to be apprehended before he could shoot anyone else. Diane Downs described the perpetrator as, "white, late-twenties, about five feet nine, 150 to 170 pounds, dark wavy hair, a stubble of beard, wearing a denim jacket and an off-colored T-shirt." Yet despite quick action by the police, despite an exhaustive search, no trace of the mystery gunman was found.

And it wasn't long before officers began to wonder whether he even existed. Something about Diane Downs's story, about her demeanor, just didn't sit right. She was too calm for one thing. Someone who had come through such a terrifying experience, losing one of her children, seeing others severely injured and not yet out of danger, would have been devastated, traumatized. Diane was calm and dry-eyed. On hearing that her middle child, Cheryl, had died, she registered no emotion. When she learned that Danny was going to make it, her response stunned medical staff. "You mean the bullet missed his heart?" she said incredulously. "Gee whiz!"

And the crime scene itself caused law officers to question her story. The stretch of highway between Marcola and Old Mohawk Roads was dark, desolate and eerie. Why, they wondered, would a young mother, with three small children in the car, stop for a total stranger in such an isolated spot?

Another cause for suspicion was the wound to Diane's arm. Those officers who'd been on the job more than a few years had seen that kind of injury before. Usually, it was self-inflicted by criminals who wanted to create the impression that they were the victim rather than the perpetrator.

All of this was, of course, conjecture. Downs had said that she'd stopped because she thought the man needed help, and that might be true. As for her demeanor, well, we all deal with grief and trauma in our own way. Better to focus on the physical evidence. Of that, there was plenty.

It was determined that the weapon used had been a .22, probably a handgun; powder burns on the children's skin suggested that the shots had been fired at extremely close range; blood spatters indicated that the shooter had fired from the driver's side of the vehicle.

This tied in with Diane Downs's story. She said that she'd been returning from visiting a co-worker, Heather Plourd. On the drive home, she'd decided that she'd take Old Mohawk Road rather than the highway because she thought it might be "fun to go sightseeing." It was just after making the turn that she spotted the man, standing in the middle of the gravel road, signaling for her to stop.

She applied the brakes and got out of the car. The stranger approached, then produced a pistol from his jacket and demanded her car keys. She refused to hand them over, whereupon he leaned in through the driver's window and fired at her children. He then reached for her, but she evaded his grasp, got into the car and got the engine started. He fired one more shot, hitting her in the arm. Then she mashed her foot down on the gas and raced away. Her only thought, she said, was to get her kids to the hospital.

The next step in the investigation was to carry out a search of Diane's home. She willingly agreed, informing officers that she kept a .38 revolver and a .22 caliber rifle there for self-protection. Neither weapon had been fired recently, but the police nonetheless took both into evidence, along with a diary.

Meanwhile, Diane's vehicle was transported to the crime lab for further investigation, and the body of Cheryl Downs went to the morgue for autopsy. Then Diane was allowed in to see her daughter, Christie, who was now out of surgery and stable. Several nurses and a police officer were present at this visit. All would later testify to Christie's strange reaction to her mother's presence. As Diane approached the bed and whispered a faint, "I love you," Christie's eyes appeared to widen in fear, while the monitor measuring her heart rate jumped from 104 beats per minute to 147.

The day after the shootings, the case was assigned to rookie Assistant DA Fred Hugi. Despite his relative inexperience, Hugi took one look at the evidence and decided that something was amiss. And those inklings of doubt only increased after he interviewed Diane Downs. Her description of the harrowing event was nonchalant, even peppered with humor at times. Not only that, but she kept making subtle enhancements to her story, as though the added details would lend credibility.

Another reason to question Diane's version of events was a piece of information gleaned from the children's father, Steve Downs. According to Downs, his former wife had not been entirely honest about her weapons cache. She also owned a .22 pistol, he said. Asked about this, Diane flatly denied ever owning such a weapon.

Hugi didn't believe her and now made finding that weapon his number one priority. But an extensive search of the area surrounding the crime scene, even sending divers to the depths of the nearby Mohawk River, did not turn it up. And there was more bad news for Hugi when doctors informed him that Christie

Downs had suffered a stroke. The child was probably the only one who could testify as to what had really happened that night. Now doctors were saying that she might never recover fully enough to do so.

Despite these setbacks, ADA Hugi was more certain than ever that Diane Downs had been the shooter. One question, though, still bothered him. Why? Why would a young mother brutally gun down her three young children? In order to find the answer, he decided to look into Diane's background and dispatched investigators Doug Welch and Paul Alton to Arizona where she'd lived until recently.

Diane had worked as a mail deliverer out of the Channing post office. Co-workers there didn't have anything particularly negative to say about her, but there were not many who had a kind word either. What emerged was a picture of a determined, yet insecure woman, a woman with a warped sense of priorities. She refused, for example, to deliver copies of Playboy magazine on her route, yet at the same time, it was common knowledge that she slept around. Steve Downs had told investigators that his former wife liked to "bed hop." In Arizona, investigators found plenty of evidence of that.

Diane's most recent beau had been one of her co-workers, Robert Knickerbocker. When the officers interviewed Knickerbocker, he said that he'd become involved with Diane shortly after her divorce from Steve Downs in 1981. She had actively pursued him, and he, knowing her reputation, had gone along, thinking that the affair would amount to nothing more than a few sexual encounters with no strings attached. Instead, he'd landed himself in a "Fatal

Attraction" situation. Diane was soon pressing him to leave his wife for her. Knickerbocker then tried to break off the affair, but Diane refused to let go.

Matters eventually came to a head when Diane insisted that he choose between her and his wife. Knickerbocker told her that he still loved his wife. After that, he confessed the affair and he and his wife were reconciled. But Diane continued to stalk him, once even confronting his wife at their home and on another occasion pounding on their front door for hours and screaming obscenities.

That was in February 1983. Not long after, Diane put in for a transfer to Oregon and moved to Springfield to be close to her parents. But she continued harassing her old boyfriend with letters and phone calls.

Knickerbocker shared two other important pieces of information with the officers. He confirmed Steve Downs's assertion that Diane had indeed owned a .22 handgun. He also provided the officers with a possible motive for the shootings.

On one occasion during the relationship, Diane had showed up to meet him with her kids in tow. Knickerbocker had left immediately, saying he didn't want to spend time with her while she was with her kids. His reason for this, he explained to the officers, was because he didn't believe that the children should be exposed to their mother's infidelities. However, Diane had interpreted it differently. She became obsessed with the idea that Knickerbocker only wanted to end the relationship because of her

children. Armed with this information, the detectives returned to
Oregon.

In June 1983, Assistant DA Hugi called a meeting of his
investigative staff to determine if they had enough to arrest Diane
Downs for murder. The conclusion was that, despite strong
circumstantial evidence, the absence of the murder weapon meant
that they probably didn't. Nonetheless, a grand jury was
assembled to hear testimony in the case.

During the nine months that those proceedings lasted, Diane
Downs became something of a media darling, appearing in
tabloids and newspapers up and down the Pacific coast. Most
media depicted her as an innocent woman who been through a
terrible ordeal and was now having her grief compounded by
being dragged through the courts. Contributing to this image,
Diane got herself pregnant by a new lover and used this in the
press. She said that she'd decided to have another child because
she missed Christie and Cheryl and Danny so much. (Christie and
Danny had been placed in foster homes by a judge.)

In February 1984, the grand jury announced its ruling. They
indicted Downs on one charge of murder, two charges of
attempted murder, and two charges of criminal assault.

The matter came to trial at the Lane County Courthouse, in
Eugene, Oregon, on May 10, 1984. By then, it was a sensation
across America, with people divided as to whether Diane Downs
had gunned down her children or not.

There were several moments of high drama during the trial, most notably when the jury was transported to the crime scene and when they were allowed to view Downs's blood-spattered Nissan Pulsar. The most dramatic interlude, though, was the testimony given by Christie Downs.

Shivering and teary-eyed, speaking in a barely audible voice, Christie was asked, "Who shot you?"

"My mom," she said simply.

After that, the case was lost to Diane Downs. Almost overnight, public opinion swung against her. She went from martyr to demon in the blink of an eye. When the jury announced its decision on June 14, 1984, no one was surprised that it was "Guilty."

Diane Downs was sentenced to life in prison, with fifty years added for using a firearm in the crime. Not long after sentence was passed, she gave birth to a daughter who she named Amy. The child was subsequently adopted.

In 1987, Downs pulled off a daring escape from the Oregon Women's Correctional Center. She remained at large for 10 days before being captured less than a mile from the prison. As a result of that escapade, she was transferred to the maximum-security Clinton Correctional Institution in New Jersey. She remains there to this day.

Danny Downs was confined to a wheelchair as a result of his injuries, while Christie made a full recovery. Both were adopted by Fred Hugi, the Assistant District Attorney who had successfully prosecuted their mother.

Delfina and Maria Gonzalez

In early January 1964, a young woman named Catalina Ortega staggered into a police station in Leon, Guanajuato, Mexico. She had a terrifying tale to tell. According to Catalina, she'd been kidnapped, beaten, tortured and forced to work as a prostitute in a brothel in nearby San Francisco del Rincon. She had managed to escape, she said, but many other girls were still being held there. Many more had been murdered.

The story sounded incredible, but one look at the unfortunate woman told police that there might some truth in it. She was obviously terrified, and it was clear that she had suffered physical abuse. She was also severely malnourished.

The cops quickly arranged a search warrant and set off for the ranch Catalina had described, an establishment run by sisters Delfina and Maria Gonzalez. What they found there shocked them and caused a sensation that reverberated throughout the whole of Mexico.

Delfina and Maria de Jesus Gonzalez were born in El Salto de Juanacatlan, in Jalisco state. Their father, Isidro Torres, was a policeman, a brutal and abusive man who was prone to abusing his power and did not spare his daughters from his violent outbursts. A favorite punishment was to lock the girls up in the local jail if they displeased him.

Given his propensity for violence it was perhaps inevitable that Isidro would overstep his authority and, after shooting to death a well-connected local man, he was forced to flee. He took his family to the village of San Francisco del Rincon (known as San Pancho to the locals) in the neighboring state of Guanajuato.

As Delfina and Maria grew older, they showed a fair bit of entrepreneurial spirit, and together with two other sisters, Carmen and Maria Luisa, they opened a number of small businesses in town. Eventually, they scraped together enough money to buy a bar in San Pancho.

The sisters no doubt thought that the saloon would to be a big money-spinner, but the takings were disappointing. Looking for other ways to make money, they hit on the idea of introducing a few "working girls" to the bar and were surprised at how lucrative it turned out to be.

Soon the Gonzalez sisters were opening a string of brothels in the area and beyond, including in Purisima del Rincon, Leon, El Salto, San Juan de los Lagos, Jalisco and San Juan del Rio. Such a vast operation needed a lot of prostitutes, and they solved this problem by employing several recruiters to scour the country for pretty young girls.

The girls would be offered jobs as waitresses in Guadalajara or Leon and, keen for a taste of the big city, most would agree. In other cases, young women were simply snatched off the street by Delfina's lover, Hermengildo Zuniga, and his army of henchmen. Once in the sisters' hands, the girls would be drugged, beaten and tortured, then forced to work in the brothels. Pretty young virgins were the most valued and would be held back for wealthy clients who would pay top dollar for unsullied "merchandise."

You might wonder how the sisters Gonzalez were able to get away with what amounted to wholesale kidnapping and slavery, but in truth it was easy. A combination of bribery, blackmail and intimidation saw to it that local law enforcement never looked in their direction.

As for the girls, they were held at Loma del Angel, a ranch that was basically a concentration camp. There they were bowed and beaten into submission, with Zuniga and Delfina Gonzalez's son, Ramon "El Tepo" Torres, serving as the muscle.

When one of the girls got pregnant, she would be beaten until she aborted. If a girl became too ill to work or failed to please the customers, she'd be murdered or starved to death. On other occasions, the other girls would be forced to beat their ailing colleague to death with clubs. The body would then be burned and buried in a mass grave.

Sick and uncooperative girls weren't the only ones to meet a nasty end. Any customer who was foolish enough to flash a wad of cash in one of the Gonzalez brothels was likely to find himself robbed and murdered.

In 1963, Ramon Torres was shot and killed during a confrontation with Jalisco police officers. Enraged by his death, Delfina ordered Zuniga to track down the officers involved and execute them, which he did. A bad mistake, as it turned out. Officers who had previously been prepared to turn a blind eye to the sisters' activities were now just waiting for an opportunity to nail them.

It came in January 1964 when Catalina Ortega escaped and went to the police. Within days, an arrest warrant had been issued. On January 14th, 1964, the police raided Loma del Angel.

Things moved quickly against the sisters now. With angry villagers gathering and threatening to lynch them, they were taken into custody. Then, as police began searching the ranch, they found dozens of filthy and emaciated women, locked up in the most appalling of conditions. Soon those women were pointing out places where bodies had been buried, and an evacuation of those areas turned up human remains. Eventually, the decomposed flesh and charred bones of at least 91 individuals were recovered from the site.

Delfina and Maria were taken to the jail at San Francisco del Rincon, then, after villagers threatened to kill them, to the Irapuato City Jail. A week later, Maria Luisa handed herself over to police in

Mexico City. (The other sister, Carmen, had died of cancer in 1958.)

The trial was as shambolic as it was sensational. Dozens of witnesses came forward to testify to the inhuman cruelty of the Gonzalez sisters. They were accused variously of murder, kidnapping and rape. Lurid testimony revealed how they'd forced young women into sexual acts with animals, how they'd dabbled in Satanism, how they'd killed and tortured and brutalized the young girls unfortunate enough to fall into their hands.

The sentences, when they were handed down, were considered lenient by most observers, 40 years in prison for each of the evil sisters.

Only one of them would survive the term of incarceration.

Delfina Gonzalez, terrified that she'd be murdered in prison, went insane and took to constant ranting and screaming. On October 17, 1968, workers doing repair work at the Irapuato prison "accidentally" dropped a bucket of cement on her head, killing her.

Maria Luisa Gonzalez died alone in her cell at Irapuato jail on November 19, 1984. By the time her body was found, it had already been partially consumed by rats.

Maria de Jesus Gonzalez was released from prison at age 64. She lived out the rest of her life in obscurity and is believed to have died of old age in 1990.

In 2002, workers clearing land for a housing development near the notorious Loma del Angel ranch found human remains in a shallow pit. The 20 individuals were determined to have died in the 1950s or 1960s and were thought to be additional victims of deadly Gonzalez sisters.

Carolyn Warmus

In the summer of 1987, a new movie hit American screens and became an instant sensation. Fatal Attraction starred Michael Douglas as a wayward husband and Glenn Close as his psychotic, obsessive lover. Their brief affair goes horribly wrong when the Glenn Close character starts stalking and threatening Douglas's family. But frightening though it was, Fatal Attraction was only fiction. In January 1989, a case occurred that had eerie similarities to the movie. Only this time, it was for real.

Carolyn Warmus was born on January 8, 1964, in Troy, Michigan. Her father was a self-made insurance millionaire named Tom Warmus, worth an estimated $150 million. As such, Carolyn lacked for nothing growing up. The Warmus marriage, though, was not a happy one, and it ended in a bitter divorce in 1972. Carolyn, just eight years old at that time, went to live with her mother. Her parents would continue a bitter struggle over custodial issues throughout her childhood.

It is difficult to know what effect these ongoing disputes had on Carolyn, but by the time she'd graduated high school and enrolled at the University of Michigan, it was clear that the attractive young woman was dealing with some issues. During her college years, she became involved in a series of relationships, always with men who were married or otherwise unattainable. None of these affairs ended well, with Carolyn accused of obsessive behavior, characterized by stalking and hiring private detectives to spy on her lovers. One of her former boyfriends even had to obtain a restraining order after she deluged his fiancée with threatening phone messages, harassed his friends, and claimed to be pregnant with his child.

Despite her somewhat tangled love life, Warmus was a diligent student who graduated from UM with a degree in psychology. Thereafter she moved to New York City, where she obtained a Master's degree in elementary education from Columbia University. In September 1987, she landed a job at Greenville Elementary in Scarsdale, New York. It was at Greenville that she met Paul Solomon, a fifth-grade teacher 15 years her senior.

Solomon was married with a teenaged daughter, but his marriage was far from solid. Both he and his wife, Betty Jeanne, had been involved in extra-marital affairs, several in Paul's case. Once the attractive, 23-year-old Carolyn set her sights on him, Solomon felt himself powerless to resist. He and Carolyn were soon lovers. For her part, Carolyn tried to insinuate herself into Solomon's family life. She regularly visited the family, trying to win Betty Jeanne's friendship and showering his 13-year-old daughter Kristan with expensive gifts.

Although Paul Solomon was deeply attracted to Carolyn, he had no intention of leaving his wife, something he'd made clear to Carolyn on several occasions. She, however, held out hope that they would one day be together. Those dreams appeared to be shattered in August 1988, when Solomon called time on their relationship.

Carolyn Warmus, of course, had been down this road before. She responded in typical fashion, resorting to obsessive behavior, pestering Solomon with calls and messages, leaving gifts and notes on his doorstep. When this didn't work, she hired a private investigator, Vincent Parco, and instructed him to dig up some dirt on Betty Jeanne in order to prove to Solomon that she was having an affair. Then she began asking Parco to procure a gun for her and nagging him to find her a silencer for the weapon.

On Sunday afternoon, January 15, 1989, Paul and Betty Jeanne Solomon were home together watching television. Kristan was away on a weekend ski trip with friends. At around 1:40 p.m., the phone in the kitchen rang. Paul answered it, and was surprised to hear Carolyn's voice on the other end of the line. He hadn't heard from Carolyn for some time, and the two of them chatted for a while before Carolyn suggested that they meet up for drinks at Treetops Restaurant, a place where they'd often rendezvoused during their affair. Paul (who admitted at the subsequent trial that he found it impossible to resist Carolyn) readily agreed. After hanging up the phone, he told Betty Jeanne that he was going bowling that night.

At about 6:30 p.m., Paul Solomon left his home to meet up with Carolyn. He drove first to the Brunswick Lanes about five miles from his apartment. He often bowled there and most of the regulars knew him, but on that evening he stayed only a short time, said hellos to several people and then left. Paul's next stop was Treetops Restaurant, situated in the Holiday Inn, just off Tuckahoe Road in Yonkers. He took a seat at the bar and ordered a drink.

Carolyn arrived at around 7:45 p.m. She joined Solomon at the bar and they had several drinks before retiring to one of the booths. They spent about two hours together, enjoying a meal and several more drinks. After leaving the restaurant, they walked to Carolyn's car in a dark corner of the parking lot. Once inside, they started kissing and Carolyn performed oral sex on Paul. They then parted, promising to meet again soon. Carolyn headed back to Manhattan, Paul to his home just a few minutes away in the Scarsdale Ridge complex.

At 11:42 p.m., a phone at the Scarsdale Police Department started jangling. The dispatcher picked up the call to hear a frantic man on the other end of the line.

"It's my wife!" the man wailed. "I think she's dead! She's not moving. She's covered with blood! Please hurry!"

Asked to identify himself, the man gave his name as Paul Solomon and said that he lived at the Scarsdale Ridge Apartments. A unit was immediately dispatched to that address and found a clearly distraught Solomon. There was blood on his hands and shirt, and the source was pretty obvious. There was a body lying face down on the floor, a pool of blood spreading out from several bullet wounds to the back and legs.

"When I got home, the first thing I heard was the TV on very loud," Solomon explained. "I walked into the living room. The lights were out and I noticed that Betty Jeanne was on the floor. I assumed she was asleep, but when I touched her, she was cold. I went and turned the lights on. I turned her over and there was blood. I thought she had fallen and hit her head."

The officers initially thought that Betty Jeanne Solomon had been the victim of a robbery gone wrong. But the scene didn't support that. There was no sign of forced entry, no suggestion of a struggle, and no evidence that anything had been stolen. Who then had killed Betty Jeanne Solomon?

Detective Richard Constantino, assigned as the lead investigator in the case, immediately suspected the husband, Paul Solomon. That theory, however, was quickly blown out of the water. Constantino was informed of a frantic call that had been made from the Solomon house at around 7:12, a woman's voice (presumed to be Betty Jeanne Solomon) screaming that someone was killing her. The call had quickly been cut off and the police had been unable to trace it, but it appeared to clear Solomon of murder. He'd been at the Brunswick Lanes at 7:12 and had spoken to several witnesses.

Crime scene investigators had meanwhile lifted four .25-caliber shell casings from the murder scene and established that Betty Jeanne had been shot at least eight times. Later, Solomon gave a formal written statement in which he admitted to being with his lover at Treetops on the night of the murder and to having sex in her car. That provided the police with a possible motive, but Solomon still had his unshakable alibi.

The following day, Constantino contacted Carolyn Warmus and asked her to   come down to the station for an interview. She readily agreed, but once there refused to answer questions without a lawyer present. The interview was immediately terminated and the investigation seemingly stalled.

Warmus's refusal to talk to the police, however, was ill-judged. By March 1989, Constantino had chased down every available lead and come up empty. Facing the prospect of his case slipping away, the detective resorted to desperate measures. In April, he got a subpoena for Warmus's telephone records, and it was through those records that he linked her to Manhattan private eye, Vincent Parco.

When detectives questioned Parco, he said that Carolyn was a former client who had hired him to check up on her boyfriend. After that work was completed, he and Carolyn had stayed in touch and she occasionally phoned him to say hello. But the investigators didn't buy that and under constant pressing, they eventually got Parco to admit that he'd obtained a gun for Carolyn, shortly before Betty Jeanne Solomon was murdered. Further probing led to an admission that he'd sent the gun over to a friend of his named George Peters, who had manufactured a silencer for the weapon.

The manufacture and sale of silencers is, of course, illegal, so investigators had plenty of leverage when they visited Peters at his machine shop in Brooklyn. He admitted making the silencer, adding that he'd test fired the .25-caliber handgun into a block of wood in his workshop. Detectives extracted four rounds from the wooden block. Ballistic tests would provide a perfect match to the bullets that had killed Betty Jeanne.

The noose was tightening around Carolyn Warmus, but the police still had one more piece of evidence to find, and it came once again from Carolyn's phone records. On January 15, she'd made a five-minute call to "Ray's Sport Shop" in North Plainfield, New Jersey. Detectives visited the shop and found four purchases of .25-caliber ammunition on the day of the murder. One had been made by a Long Island woman named Liisa Kattai, who had given her New York State driver's license as proof of I.D.

Kattai, as it turned out, had never visited North Plainfield, New Jersey, and had certainly never purchased ammunition from Ray's Sport Shop. She did, however, provide an explanation as to how her I.D. might have been used for the purchase. Her license had been either lost or stolen while she was working a job that summer. It had since been reported to the Department of Motor Vehicles and replaced. Asked whether she knew a woman named Carolyn Warmus, Kattai said that she did. Carolyn had been one of her co-workers during her summer employment.

The police now had evidence linking Carolyn to the murder weapon and to the purchase of ammunition on the day of the murder.

On February 2, 1990, Carolyn Warmus was indicted for the murder of Betty Jeanne Solomon, sparking a media frenzy. Warmus was portrayed as a "Sex Tigress," "A Woman Obsessed," and a "Black Widow." Comparisons were also drawn between her and Alex Forrest, the character played by Glenn Close in Fatal Attraction.

The trial opened on January 14, 1991, in a tenth-floor courtroom in White Plains, New York. It ended on April 27, with a hung jury. Carolyn was free - at least for now. The second time around she would not be so lucky. On May 21, 1992, the jury delivered a unanimous guilty verdict. The judge then sentenced her to the maximum term of twenty-five years to life.

Carolyn Warmus is currently serving her time at the Bedford Prison for Women. She will be eligible for parole in 2017. By then, she will be 53 years old.

Christine & Lea Papin

On the evening of February 2, 1933, a prominent lawyer from the French city of Le Mans was returning from a business trip. Rene Lancelin had arranged to meet his wife Marie and daughter Genevieve for dinner at a friend's house, so he went directly there. He was surprised and slightly annoyed to find that his wife and daughter had not yet arrived.

An hour passed with no sign of the women. Lancelin, growing more agitated by the moment, then tried phoning his residence but got no reply. Eventually, he returned home, to find the place in almost complete darkness. The only illumination came from a candle in the attic room occupied by the family's maids, Christine and Lea Papin.

M. Lancelin tried his key in the lock and found that the front door was bolted from the inside. He pounded on the door and called out for the maids, drawing no response. Entering through a window was out of the question. They were all closed and shuttered. The back door too was bolted internally. His frustration by now had

turned to dread that something was terribly wrong, Lancelin went
for the police. He returned a short while later with an inspector
and two burly gendarmes who were able to force the back door.
What awaited them inside was a massacre worse than any they
had ever encountered.

Madame Lancelin and her daughter lay sprawled on the first floor.
Both had been hideously mutilated, their heads so severely
battered that they were barely recognizable as human. And that
wasn't even the worst of it. The women had been slashed and cut,
their eyes gouged out and left lying on the floor; blood spattered
every surface of the room, in some places reaching as high as the
ceiling. Nearby lay the implements of murder: a hammer, two
knives and a badly battered pewter vase. The killers, it appeared,
had directed most of their attack at the heads of the victims,
although Genevieve Lancelin had suffered deep cuts to her legs
and buttocks.

There was quite obviously nothing that could be done for the
victims, so the police officers continued up to the maids' room, half
expecting to find a similar scene of carnage there. What they found
instead was Christine and Lea, huddled up in bed together, naked
but for the kimonos they each wore.

The sisters were bundled into a police van and driven to the local
gendarmerie, where they offered a full confession. The older of the
two, Christine, did most of the talking. She said that the murders
stemmed from a petty dispute that had flared up between the
sisters and their employer a month earlier. At that time, Lea had
damaged an iron and Mme. Lancelin had told her that the cost of
repairing it would have to be deducted from her wages. That had

not sat well with the sisters, but they kept their peace until February 2, the day of the murders. Then, Lea had again been using the iron, when the poorly repaired instrument had fused the electricity in the chateaux.

Mme. Lancelin and her daughter had been out at the time, and the Papin sisters had spent the afternoon fretting over what would happen when they returned. Their mistress was a cruel and uncompromising woman, Christine said, so they expected the punishment to be harsh. Sure enough, Madame was furious. First, she slapped Lea. Then she dropped her shopping and instructed the sisters to carry the bags to the first floor. As they reached the landing, she attacked again, but this time, Christine fought back, tackling Mme. Lancelin to the ground and gouging at her eyes. Genevieve tried to go to the aid of her mother, but Lea attacked her with fists and nails.

The sisters soon had the upper hand, their employers writhing on the floor, screaming in pain and begging for mercy. Christine had entirely removed both of Mme Lancelin's eyes, gouging them out with her fingernails. Lea had inflicted similar wounds on Genevieve; one of her eyes had been removed and now lay on the floor like a bizarre, blood-soaked grape.

But still, Christine wasn't finished. She rushed downstairs to the kitchen, returning with a hammer and two knives. The sisters then fell upon their helpless victims, beating and slashing, continuing their assault long after Mme. Lancelin and Genevieve were dead. Eventually, they broke off the attack. Then they went downstairs to bolt the doors and shuttered the windows. Afterwards, they returned to their quarters where they stripped off and washed the blood from their bodies. Finally, they slipped into bed and awaited the inevitable arrival of the police.

As news of the horrific double murder began leaking out, the whole of France was horrified and captivated by the story. Newspapers blared lurid headlines about "Murderous Maids," and those who had domestic staff of their own were genuinely afraid that this might be a trend, an uprising of the working class against the bourgeois. Many domestics suddenly found themselves treated with new respect.

The Papin sisters, meanwhile, were sent to prison to await trial. They were kept separately, something that caused them far greater distress than the horrific double murder they'd committed. Christine was particularly affected. She spent much of her time screaming, cursing and howling like a banshee. She cried constantly to be with Lea. On other occasions, she rolled and writhed on her cell floor. Eventually, after she tried to pluck her own eyes out, the authorities relented and allowed her to see her sister. When the guards tried to separate them at the end of the visit, they clung so fiercely to each other that it took five men to separate them. They would not see each other again until their trial.

On September 30, 1933, Christine and Lea Papin appeared at the Palace of Justice in Le Mans, charged with two counts of murder. Such was the public feeling against the sisters that the authorities feared an attempt might be made to assassinate them. Access to the courtroom was therefore strictly controlled, with vast crowds gathered in the square outside.

The testimony was shocking, but the sisters made no attempt to deny any of it, only objecting when it was suggested that they had been involved in an incestuous lesbian relationship. Christine admitted nonchalantly to gouging out Mme. Lancelin's eyes with her fingernails and to bludgeoning her repeatedly with a hammer. She also admitted that she instructed Lea to do the same. At this point, someone in the public gallery rose and shouted out, "Death to the sisters!" He was promptly removed from the courtroom.

But death was indeed the sentence passed down by the judge, at least in the case of Christine. Lea, who was considered to have been incited to murder by her older sister, was sentenced to ten years at hard labor.

Christine's sentence was later commuted to life imprisonment, which was standard practice in France in the case of female killers. She did not, however, adapt well to prison life. Severely depressed over her separation from her beloved Lea, she refused to eat and her condition rapidly deteriorated. Eventually, she was moved to an asylum in the town of Rennes, where she died in 1937 of cachexia, literally a wasting away of the body.

Lea, on the other hand, did well in prison. She'd always been a quiet, mild-mannered girl when not under the influence of her sister, and her good behavior earned her an early release after eight years. Thereafter, she moved to Nantes, where she adopted a new identity and found work as a chambermaid. There are differing stories as to her ultimate fate. One says that she died in 1982 at the age of 70, another that she lived into her nineties and passed away in 2001.

Joanna Dennehy

The murders were among the most brutal in the annals of British crime, made all the more remarkable because the killer was not some hulking monster but a petite, 30-year-old mother of two named Joanna Dennehy.

Born into a respectable, middle-class family in 1982, Joanna Dennehy grew up in a stable household in St Albans, in Hertfordshire, England. She was a bright child who did well in school and dreamed of becoming a lawyer. She was seldom a problem to her parents. However, by the time Joanna reached her teens, all of that had changed. She began experimenting with drugs and alcohol and developed a disconcerting habit of slashing at her skin with razor blades. Joanna was also suspended from school for drinking and for stealing, and she was committed for psychiatric evaluation on several occasions.

Joanna's long-suffering parents tolerated all of these destructive behaviors, but they drew the line when their 15-year-old daughter started a relationship with a 21-year-old man. Given the choice

between ending the affair and leaving her parents' home, Joanna
chose the latter.

Joanna's new paramour was a man named John Treanor. Like
Joanna, he was unemployed and a drug user. The pair spent a year
living on the streets before they eventually found a place to stay, in
a shared house in Luton, Bedfordshire. Shortly thereafter, they
were forced to flee to nearby Milton Keynes, after they tipped off
the police about a drug dealer operating out of the house.

In 1999, when she was 17, Joanna fell pregnant. As someone who
had always insisted that she didn't want kids, the news left her
devastated, moody and angry. After the birth of her daughter, she
began drinking heavily and snorting cocaine. She also started an
affair with a neighbor. When John found out, he packed up his
daughter and moved to his parents' home in Norfolk. Joanna,
however, followed and begged him to take her back. She promised
to clean up her act, and she did, even finding a job picking
vegetables at a nearby farm. But it wasn't long before she started
drinking again. And when she was drunk, she became violent. John
was often seen sporting cuts and bruises and black eyes. Unable to
tolerate any more of Joanna's erratic behavior, he left again. This
time he stayed away for eighteen months, but eventually, and
against his better judgment, he took her back.

In 2003, the couple set up home in the town of Wisbech,
Cambridgeshire, where their drunken rows soon became
legendary, with police called to intervene on several occasions.
Neighbors also suspected that they were selling drugs out of their
house, even if the police found no evidence of this illicit trade
when they carried out a raid in 2005. A year later, Joanna was

forced to cut down on her drinking when she found herself pregnant with her second child.

A familiar pattern now followed. Unwilling or unable to cope with the demands of motherhood, Joanna began hitting the bottle again. Often, she'd disappear for weeks on end. John heard rumors that she was involved in a lesbian relationship with a woman named Charmaine and that she was working as a prostitute to fund her drink and drug habits. But even that was preferable to having Joanna at home. By this time, she was drinking two liters of vodka a day, slicing her neck and arms to shreds with razor blades and taking out her frustrations on John and the kids. Eventually, after a frightening episode in which she pulled a knife and started ripping at the carpets, he left again -- this time for good.

With John out of the picture Joanna moved to Peterborough, where she soon had another lover, a giant of a man known as Gary Stretch. Standing at 7-foot-3, Stretch was a small-time criminal who was instantly besotted with Joanna and her fanciful stories about the murders and other crimes she had committed. Joanna, however, did not share his devotion. She continued to play the field, carrying on sexual relationships with both male and female lovers.

Lucasz Slaboszewski was not one of those lovers, but he hoped to be. The 31-year-old Pole had recently moved to the UK to look for work and had met Joanna in the town center. Like Stretch, he was attracted to Joanna, so when she invited him to her apartment on March 19, 2013, he immediately accepted. Once there, he and Joanna talked and drank vodka and appeared to hit it off. When Joanna asked if she could blindfold him, Lucasz agreed, thinking it was the start of some sort of sex game. He could not have been more wrong. As soon as the blindfold dropped over his eyes, Dennehy picked up a knife and plunged it into his chest, piercing his heart and killing him instantly.

Dennehy's impulsive act of violence had left her with a problem, though. She now had a body to get rid of, and she lacked the strength to even lift it, let alone carry it from the building. A phone call to Gary Stretch quickly resolved that. He arrived at Dennehy's apartment with a friend, Leslie Layton, and soon they had Slaboszewski's body stashed away in a garbage bin behind an adjacent apartment block. A couple of days later, he and Layton moved the corpse from its hiding place and drove into the countryside outside Peterborough, where they unceremoniously dumped it in a ditch.

Dennehy has never revealed her motive for killing Lucasz Slaboszewski, but given subsequent events, it is safe to assume that she was thrilled by the act of murder. Why else would she have repeated it just nine days later?

Fifty-six-year-old John Chapman lived in the same building as Dennehy. A veteran of the Falklands War, Chapman was known as a loner, but on March 28, Dennehy managed to talk herself into his apartment. The two of them started drinking heavily until Chapman eventually passed out. Then Dennehy produced her knife and inflicted six vicious stab wounds to his chest and neck. John Chapman never stood a chance. After he was dead, Dennehy called on her trusted disposal team. Chapman's body ended up in the ditch beside Lucasz Slaboszewski.

Within hours of murdering Chapman, Dennehy was on the hunt again. The victim she chose was Kevin Lee, her landlord and sometime lover. Lee was lured to Dennehy's apartment with the promise of sex. There, he and Joanna indulged in a game they had played often in the past, with Joanna dressing him up in one of her dresses. Then, when his back was turned, she struck. Launching a frenzied knife attack. Gary Stretch received another call that night, and he and his accomplice Layton dutifully carried Kevin Lee's body to another roadside ditch, some seven miles from where the other two victims lay.

Joanna Dennehy had now killed three men in the space of just 10 days, her only motive the pleasure she apparently derived from the act of murder. But she had miscalculated in killing Kevin Lee. Unlike her first two victims, who had no close ties, Lee was immediately missed. A search was launched after Lee's family reported his disappearance to the police. Later that day, his body was discovered in the ditch where it had been dumped. Dennehy was soon flagged as a "person of interest." However, when police called to question her, they found that she had fled the county with her lover, Gary Stretch.

On April 2, 2013, Dennehy and Stretch showed up at the home of a criminal associate of his in Hereford. They had some stolen goods to sell, and the friend, Mark Lloyd, agreed to help. The trio set off in Stretch's car, but Lloyd was stunned when Dennehy started boasting about the three murders she had committed and joking about how many more she was going to kill. "I'm a killer," she said. "I want my fun, I want to have my fun, I want to do nine."

Lloyd wasn't sure whether to believe Joanna's boasts or not, but any doubts he might have had were soon banished in horrific fashion. As he sat in the back seat, Stretch suddenly brought the vehicle to a halt and pointed out an old man walking along the sidewalk. In the next moment, Dennehy sprang from the vehicle and sprinted towards the man, 64-year-old Robin Bereza. Before Bereza had a chance to react, she had drawn her knife and plunged it into his shoulder. He collapsed to the ground immediately, an action that probably saved his life. Believing that she'd struck a killing blow, Joanna ran back to the car. Moments later they were racing away from the scene with Dennehy and Stretch roaring laughter, and Lloyd terror struck in the back seat.

And still Dennehy's bloodlust wasn't sated. Nine minutes after stabbing Robin Bereza, she spotted 57-year-old John Rogers walking his dog along a bicycle path. After ordering Stretch to pull over, she got out of the car and launched a frenzied attack on Rogers, stabbing him over 40 times before taking his dog and returning to the car. John Rogers was left bleeding on the path where he was found minutes later by a passerby. Both he and Robin Bereza would survive to identify their attacker, describing the distinctive star tattoo she had on her face.

By now, the bodies of Lucasz Slaboszewski and John Chapman had been found, and the police had identified Dennehy as the common denominator in the attacks. A warrant was issued for her arrest, and she and Stretch were picked up days later. Charged with three counts of murder and two of attempted murder on May 8, 2013, Dennehy stunned her accusers by bursting out into a rendition of "Singing in the Rain."

By the time Dennehy's case came to trial in November 2013, she had lost none of her good spirits. She stood smirking in the dock and appeared totally oblivious to the pain and heartache she had caused. Ignoring the advice of her legal counsel, she entered guilty pleas to all the charges against her, saying that she "just wanted to get it over with."

Joanna Dennehy was sentenced to a whole life term, becoming only the third woman in British history to receive that sentence (the others were notorious multiple murderers Rosemary West and Myra Hindley). Gary Stretch was also sentenced to life in prison, while Leslie Layton got 14 years for his involvement. Mark Lloyd, who had been in the car when Dennehy attacked Robin Bereza and John Rogers, was not charged with any crime.

Andrea Yates

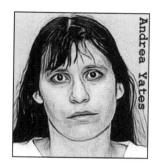

The woman on the other end of the line was adamant. "I need a police officer."

"What's your name?" the 911 dispatcher wanted to know.

"Andrea Yates," the caller said. "I need a police officer."

"Are you having a disturbance, Mrs. Yates? Are you ill?"

"Um, yes, I'm ill."

"Do you need an ambulance?"

"No, I need a police officer. Yes, send an ambulance."

"Can you tell me what's wrong?"

"I just need a police officer."

Dispatchers working the lines at 911 stations across the country deal with this type of call all the time. The caller is cryptic, reticent, maddeningly vague. It may be a hoax and it may not be. There's just no way of knowing. Still, every call has to be actioned, even if it ends up diverting resources from genuine cases. And so the dispatcher directed a police cruiser to the Houston address provided. After a moment's thought, she dispatched an ambulance as well. Those first responders were about to walk in on one of the most infamous crime scenes in US history.

Andrea Yates was born Andrea Pia Kennedy in Houston, Texas, on July 2, 1964. Her mother was a German national, her father the son of Irish immigrants. She was raised Catholic and attended Milby High School in Houston, where she captained the swim team and served as an officer in the National Honor Society. In 1982, she graduated as class valedictorian. Thereafter, she enrolled on a two-year pre-nursing program at the University of Houston, completing her nursing diploma at the University of Texas School of Nursing. She'd later work as a registered nurse at the University of Texas M.D. Anderson Cancer Center.

So far, everything in Andrea Kennedy's life appeared to be well on track, give or take a few brief bouts of depression and bulimia during her high school years and an ingrained shyness that meant she did not go out on her first date until she was 23 years old. Then, in 1989, Andrea struck up a conversation with a young man who lived in her apartment building. His name was Russell Yates and he was two months her junior.

Nursing a broken heart from a recent relationship failure, Andrea felt herself drawn to Rusty, and before long they were dating and had moved in together. A staunch Christian who adhered to the Quiverful doctrine, Rusty soon introduced Andrea to his beliefs, which included the idea that couples should have as many children as possible. When they eventually married, on April 17, 1993, they announced to wedding guests that they planned on doing just that.

Over the next eight years, the Yateses would be good to their word, producing five offspring – four boys and a girl. Faced with the task of raising such a large brood, Andrea gave up her nursing career and became a stay-at-home mom. She and Rusty had already taken the decision that the children would be home schooled, so Andrea had plenty to keep her busy. However, from the time that her second son, John, was born in December 1995, friends and family began to notice changes in her behavior. The one-time fitness fanatic stopped jogging and swimming, she became increasingly reclusive, her family barely saw her and the children.

In 1996, Rusty got a job in Florida and the family moved for a year to Seminole. When they returned to Houston in 1997, he made an unusual choice as regards his family's living arrangements, buying a 350-square-foot, renovated bus which became their permanent home. That same year, a fourth child, Luke, was born, making conditions extremely cramped. It was around this time that the first worrying signs of Andrea's insanity began to surface.

Rusty and Andrea had, at the time, been attending church services given by a traveling preacher named Michael Woroniecki, the same man from whom Rusty had purchased the bus. Woroniecki's brand of religion was straight out of the fire-and-brimstone Old Testament. A core doctrine was that bad mothers who did not educate their children in the ways of the Lord were going straight to hell, dragging their offspring behind them. Both Rusty and Andrea bought into this bizarre teaching. Andrea, however, took it quite literally and began to fret over the harm she might be doing to her children's immortal souls.

On June 16, 1999, Andrea called Rusty at work and begged him to come home. He found her huddled in a corner, shaking uncontrollably and chewing on her fingers. The following day, she was admitted to Houston's Methodist Hospital after she swallowed a fistful of pills in an apparent suicide attempt. Transferred to the hospital's psychiatric unit, she was diagnosed with a serious depressive disorder. However, just over a week later, she was given a prescription for an antidepressant and released. Rusty's medical insurance for psychiatric treatment had run out.

Thus began a downward spiral, delivering Andrea Yates closer and closer to the gates of madness. At home, she refused to take her medication, she began slashing at her arms with a blade, she became obsessed with the idea that there was video surveillance equipment hidden around the house, watching her every move, she was convinced that cartoon characters on the TV were talking to her. Significantly, she also began to neglect her children, refusing to feed them because she said that they were eating too much. Rusty, of course, was aware of his wife's offbeat behavior, but he failed to mention it to Andrea's psychiatrist, Dr. Eileen Starbranch, during their weekly sessions. Then, on July 20, 1999, matters came to a head. Andrea put a knife to her throat and begged her husband to let her kill herself.

That episode saw Andrea back in the hospital, where she remained in a catatonic state for ten days. During that time, she was injected with various drugs and showed a positive response to a particular anti-psychotic medication, Haldol. The next few days saw an extraordinary improvement, giving Dr. Starbranch hope that she might, at last, have found a solution to Andrea's problems. But the doctor was less than enthused when Rusty confided in him that he and Andrea wanted to have another child. She strongly advised against it, saying that the stress of a pregnancy, childbirth, and possible post-natal depression would have a detrimental effect on Andrea's condition. Rusty said that he understood, and Andrea was discharged with a prescription for Haldol.

The months that followed were the happiest that the Yates family had experienced since their return from Florida. At the urging of Andrea's family, Rusty reluctantly sold the bus and bought a home in the suburbs. Under the effects of Haldol, Andrea's condition showed a marked improvement. She began swimming and jogging again. She cooked and baked for her family and became the loving, caring mother that she had been. She even began socializing with old friends.

Rusty, however, was still determined that Andrea should have another baby. Eventually, she grew tired of his pushing, and in March of 2000 she stopped taking her Haldol. On November 30, 2000, the couple's fifth child and first daughter, Mary, was born. And Dr. Starbranch's warnings appeared unwarranted as Andrea seemed to respond well to the birth and to the responsibilities of raising an infant.

But who knew the fragility of Andrea's mental state? One minor catalyst was all it would take to tip her over the edge again. And when that catalyst arrived, it was anything but minor. On March 12, 2001, Andrea's father died, throwing her into a renewed state of depression. She stopped talking, began self-mutilating, refused food and water and stopped caring for her infant daughter. She refused all activity, in fact, other than frantically reading the Bible.

By the end of March, Andrea was back in hospital, this time under the care of a different psychiatrist, Dr. Mohammed Saeed. She was briefly returned to her previous drug regimen, but Dr. Saeed was not as convinced as his predecessor about the benefits of Haldol and the medication was discontinued. Shortly thereafter, Andrea was discharged, only to return two months later with very similar symptoms. This time, she stayed ten days before being released without medication. Her doctor insisted that Andrea was not psychotic and that the drugs would, therefore, be of no benefit to her. He recommended that Rusty schedule an appointment for her with a psychologist. He also warned Rusty that she should not be left unsupervised.

On Wednesday, June 20, Rusty Yates left for work at his normal time. Over the prior two days, he had followed Dr. Saeed's instructions to the letter. He'd arranged for his mother, Dora Yates, to arrive at the house before he left, thus ensuring that Andrea was never left alone. But he'd quickly tired of that routine and decided that Andrea needed some time on her own (to gain some independence, he'd later tell police). So on this day, he phoned

Dora and told her to arrive at the house an hour later than usual, leaving Andrea alone with the children for that hour. He could not have imagined the consequences of that reckless decision.

As soon as Rusty was out of the door, Andrea went to the bathroom and filled the tub with water. Then she brought her children in one by one, starting with 3-year-old Paul, then Luke, 2, and John, 5. The boys were held under water until they drowned, barely putting up a struggle as they were systematically murdered by their mother. Then, Andrea calmly carried their bodies to the bedroom where she tucked them into bed as though they were sleeping.

The next to die was 6-month-old Mary, who succumbed within seconds. Andrea had not yet removed the baby's body from the water when her oldest, Noah, arrived and asked his mother what was going on. Then he spotted Mary's body in the tub and, perhaps realizing the horrific truth, the seven-year-old turned and ran. Andrea, however, was faster. She caught her son just before he reached the front door. Noah was dragged, kicking and screaming, back to the bathroom. He was forced into the tub where the body of his dead sister still floated, face down. Noah fought desperately, twice coming up for air before his mother eventually ended his young life. Then, Andrea removed Mary from the water, carried her to the bedroom, and she laid her to rest beside her brothers. With Noah's little corpse still floating in the tub, she walked calmly to the phone and dialed 911.

There was never any doubt as to who was responsible for the mass killing, but Andrea nonetheless made it easy for investigators by offering a full confession. She said that she'd been thinking about killing her children for two years. "It was the seventh deadly sin," she said. "My children weren't righteous. They stumbled because I was evil. The way I was raising them, they could never be saved. They were doomed to perish in the fires of hell." She later told a prison psychiatrist that Satan had influenced her children and made them more disobedient.

Andrea Yates went on trial in March 2002, with her attorney pleading her not guilty by reason of insanity. After much debate over the M'Naghten Rules and the Irresistible Impulse Test, the jury rejected that plea and found her guilty of five counts of murder. However, they decided against imposing the death penalty that the prosecution had asked for and opted instead for life imprisonment with no parole for 40 years. That sentence was reversed on appeal in January 2005, when Yates was found to meet the legal definition for insanity and committed to Kerrville State Hospital, a high-security mental health facility.

In 2012, it was revealed that Yates's attorneys had filed a motion to allow her a two-hour furlough each Sunday so that she could attend church services. "She would like to get back to church where God and Christianity can play a positive role in her life," the application stated.

Dana Sue Gray

Alice Williams and Norma Davis were friends. The two elderly ladies lived in a quiet gated community in Canyon Lake, California, and usually checked in with each other regularly. So when Alice hadn't heard from Norma for a few days, she became concerned. The community they lived in was safe, but at 87 years old, Norma might easily have fallen and hurt herself. When Norma failed to answer her phone, Alice decided to check on her.

At around 9 o'clock on the morning of February 14, 1994, Alice knocked on Norma's door. Getting no reply, she waited a few moments and then knocked again. The house remained deathly silent. Her concern growing, Alice turned the handle and found the door unlocked. This, too, worried her. Norma was security conscious. Certain now that her friend had met with an accident, Alice entered. She called out her friend's name and got no reply. Then she began climbing the stairs.

It was in the upper den that Alice found her friend. Norma was seated in a chair in her usual spot, a blanket drawn over her feet.

At first Alice thought she was sleeping, but as her eyes adjusted to the light, she could make out the wooden handles of two knives. One protruded from Norma's neck, the other from her chest. Alice staggered down the stairs and called 911.

It did not take long for police and emergency personnel to arrive. As detectives began processing the scene they immediately formed a number of impressions. The attack was vicious, the victim stabbed eleven times, her throat slashed so deeply that her head was nearly severed. This pointed to a personal motive, perhaps a vendetta. Coupled with the fact that there had been no forced entry into the home and that the victim had neither been robbed nor raped, detectives believed that the killer was most likely an acquaintance or family member. One interesting clue left at the scene was the bloody imprint of a sneaker. The print was small, leading the police to conclude that it had been made by a woman. Yet they did not believe that it belonged to the killer. A murder this brutal could not have been committed by a woman, surely?

Detectives were still working on the premise that Norma Davis had known her killer when they began questioning her friends and family. But if they'd hoped that the killer was among them and would somehow give himself up, they were disappointed. Everyone they spoke to seemed genuinely distraught at Norma's death. The active 87-year-old had been universally loved. No one could think of any person who might have wanted to harm her.

Two weeks after the murder of Norma Davis, friends and family of June Roberts phoned to congratulate her on her 66th birthday. When their calls went unanswered, three friends drove to her mobile home on Big Tee Drive in Sun City, California. There they found June's golf cart standing on the lawn, a bunch of keys that included her house key hanging from the ignition. Letting themselves in, the friends found June lying on the floor in the den, an overturned chair partially covering her body. It appeared from her terrible injuries that she'd been battered to death, a heavy wine decanter the likely murder weapon.

As in the case of Norma Davis, there was no sign of forced entry into the home, leading investigators to the belief that June had known her killer. Again there was no evidence of rape or robbery and police were at a loss as to the motive. As news of a second brutal murder was picked up by the media, the authorities moved quickly to quell speculation that there was a serial killer in the area, preying on elderly residents. The M.O. of the two crimes was significantly different, a media spokesman insisted, since one victim had been stabbed and the other bludgeoned to death.

But this assertion would soon be proved incorrect. Norma Davis had been strangled as well as stabbed, and the autopsy on June Roberts would determine that she had not died from the blows to her head as first believed. She'd been strangled to death with a length of telephone cord. Perhaps the serial killer theory was not that farfetched after all.

The police had still not admitted a link between the murders when they had another bizarre crime to deal with. On March 10, 1994, an attractive blonde woman of about 40 walked into The Main Street Trading Post, an antiques store in Lake Elsinore, California. She told the clerk, 57-year-old Dorinda Hawkins, that she was looking for picture frames. Dorinda let her browse, even allowing her into the small workshop at the back of the store. She could not have imagined what would happen next.

As Dorinda stood with her back to the customer, she felt something suddenly pulled tight around her neck. Twisting around she saw that the customer had a length of yellow nylon rope twisted around her throat and was throttling her. Dorinda tried to fight back but the woman, despite standing only 5-foot-2 was remarkably strong. She tried begging and the woman responded by speaking to her in a calm soothing voice, telling her to relax and calm down. The last thing Dorinda remembered was the woman's cold blue eyes watching her as her struggles weakened and she blacked out.

The sound of a jangling telephone roused Dorinda from unconsciousness. Her throat throbbed and felt raw and swollen. She noticed by the clock on the wall that she'd been out for forty minutes. Staggering to her feet, Dorinda walked towards the phone which had by now stopped ringing. She picked up the receiver and dialed 911. Dorinda Hawkins had just survived an encounter with a serial killer.

At first the police did not link the attack to the two murders. Dorinda was younger than the other victims, and the motive in this case had obviously been robbery. Twenty-five dollars had been taken from the register, and Dorinda's purse was also missing from her bag. After being treated, Dorinda worked with a police artist to draw up a composite sketch. The police would soon have a suspect to compare that sketch against.

On March 15, an employee at June Roberts's bank phoned Mrs. Roberts's daughter to report suspicious activity on her credit card. The card had been used after Mrs. Roberts's death. As police questioned staff at the stores where the card was used, a familiar theme began to emerge. All of them described a petite blonde woman with shoulder-length hair, a dead ringer for the woman who had attacked Dorinda Hawkins. Further inquiries gave the police a name, a former registered nurse named Dana Sue Gray. Gray was placed under surveillance, and the police noted with interest that since the composite sketch had appeared in the local papers, she'd cut her hair short and dyed it red. They also learned that Gray had known both Norma Davis and June Roberts. Armed with this evidence, the police pulled Gray in for questioning on June 16. That same day, another elderly woman was found bludgeoned to death in her home.

Dora Beebe, 87, had failed to turn up for a lunch date with a male acquaintance. Acutely aware of the recent murders in the area, he'd gone to her house to check on her. He'd found the door unlocked and Mrs. Beebe dead on the bathroom floor. Even by the standards of the previous murders, this one was incredibly brutal. The elderly woman had been battered to death with a clothes iron, the attack so vicious that when the body was removed to the morgue, the victim's shape could still be seen on the floor, outlined in blood.

The police meanwhile had executed a search warrant on the home that Gray shared with her boyfriend and his 5-year-old son. They unearthed a wealth of evidence including clothes, jewelry and perfume bought with the victims' credit cards. They also found June Roberts's bank book, showing a $2,000 withdrawal made on the day Mrs. Roberts was killed. It would later emerge that Gray had gone on a shopping spree immediately after the murder, treating herself to a perm, beauty treatments and an expensive lunch. She'd also bought clothes, perfume, liquor and gourmet foods, as well as toys for her boyfriend's son. The child had, in fact, accompanied Gray to Mrs. Roberts's home, waiting in the car while Gray was inside, stabbing and throttling the old lady.

Under interrogation, Gray offered a ludicrous explanation for how she'd come into possession of June Roberts's credit card. She said that she'd visited Mrs. Roberts at her home and found her murdered. Rather than calling the police, she'd rifled through the elderly woman's purse and taken her credit card to go on a shopping spree. "I get desperate to buy things," she explained. "Shopping puts me at rest. I'm lost without it." It was a story that the police were never likely to believe.

Dana Sue Gray went on trial for murder on March 10, 1995. She initially entered an insanity plea but, faced with the prospect of execution, she struck a deal and admitted to killing June Roberts and Dora Beebe. No charges were brought in the Davis murder due to lack of evidence. She is also suspected of three other murders in Riverside and San Diego. Gray is currently incarcerated at the California Women's Prison in Chowchilla, where she will remain for the rest of her natural life.

Kanae Kijima

Naoki Yasuda had signed up for the internet dating site more in hope than expectation. He didn't see why any attractive, single woman would need to resort to such means in order to attract a partner. And if such women did, he couldn't see why they'd be interested in a shy, lifelong bachelor like him. Still he was lonely and desperate for female company, so he posted up his details and, to his surprise, soon had a response.

The woman's name was Kanae Kijima and she was just what Naoki was looking for, someone who described herself as a homebody interested in a serious relationship. At 34, she was 12 years younger than Naoki and, if her picture was anything to go by, quite pretty. A date was quickly set up at a local restaurant.

Naoki was somewhat disappointed at his first sighting of Kanae. She was considerably plainer and sturdier than the flattering picture she'd posted on the dating site. But those initial reservations were soon swept away once they got talking. Kanae was kind and soft-spoken and attentive, and she seemed genuinely

interested in starting a serious relationship. A few more dates and
the pair were talking about setting up home together. In
September 2009, Kanae moved out of her modest Tokyo
apartment and into Naoki's house in nearby Chiba Prefecture.

Over the next three weeks, Naoki could hardly believe his luck at
landing such a gem. His new partner was an attentive and loving
companion, a spectacular cook and an extremely diligent
housekeeper. There were three cooked meals a day and cups of tea
delivered at regular intervals without him having to ask. The home
was kept spotless without him having to lift a finger to help. Even
after such a short courtship, Naoki began thinking seriously about
asking Kanae to be his wife. She seemed almost too good to be
true.

Then, on September 21, after three blissful weeks of cohabitation,
a bombshell was dropped on Naoki's newfound happiness. The
police arrived to take Kanae into custody. Bewildered, Naoki asked
about the charges. The answer stunned him. Kanae had been
meeting men on internet chat sites, drugging and then robbing
them. And that wasn't the worst of it. Four men had died. Kanae
Kijima, it appeared, was a new breed of serial killer, an internet
Black Widow.

At first, Naoki refused to believe the allegations. Kanae had
seemed so genuine, so caring, so trustworthy. But as the details of
the case came to light, he was forced to reassess his position. His
loving companion, it appeared, was a fraudster of epic
proportions. She'd been at this for a while, defrauding dozens of
men while posing as a prospective marriage partner, a home-
helper or a therapist. According to police reports, she preyed

mainly on lonely middle-aged men, who she found by trawling konkatsu (marriage-hunting) websites. Her little enterprise had netted her 200m yen ($1.8m) in just a couple of years. Naoki Yasuda had been lucky to escape with his life.

Kanae Kijima's first victim was Sadao Fukuyama. The 70-year-old was the manager of a recycling shop, a thrifty, careful man who was said to have a healthy suspicion of strangers. And yet, Fukuyama was no match for Kijima's persuasive wiles. After luring the elderly man via a dating site, she'd spun him a tale of woe. She had been a promising pianist, she said, but had been forced to give up her studies after her parents were killed in a plane crash, leaving her destitute. Her greatest wish was to complete her music degree. Fukuyama, so careful in his pecuniary affairs, was apparently taken in. He handed over 3.2 million yen ($30,000) to cover Kijima's tuition fees. Then, a couple of months into the relationship, he went even further, handing over his bank card and PIN number. Kijima then preceded to drain his account of 74 million yen ($680,000).

Sadao Fukuyama was found dead at his home on August 6, 2007. Because of his advanced age, the police did not suspect foul play at the time, although they'd later have cause to revise that assumption.

The next man to fall victim to the heartless killer was even older than Sadao Fukuyama. Kenzo Ando was an 80-year-old invalid who Kijima contacted via a website advertising for home carers. Posing as a nurse, Kijima insinuated herself into the pensioner's life and managed to coax his bank card and PIN number out of him. She then drugged Ando and set his house on fire, hoping that the blaze would obliterate the evidence. However, the fire department was able to extinguish the flames before they could consume Mr. Ando's body. His bloodstream was found to contain traces of a sedative. Meanwhile, a check on the deceased's financial affairs revealed that 1.8 million yen ($20,000) had been withdrawn from his bank account in the days leading up to his death.

Not all of Kanae Kijima's victims ended up dead. The lucky ones were simply duped out of their money before the heavyset temptress left them in the lurch and moved on to new targets. However, she did not hesitate to kill if a mark cottoned on to her game or perhaps demanded the repayment of a "loan."

A typical case was that of 53-year-old Takao Terada, found dead of carbon monoxide poisoning in his Tokyo home in February 2009. Kijima had reeled Terada in by telling him a sob story about a cake shop that she had planned on opening. At the last moment, she said, her backer had pulled out, leaving her in the lurch and deep in debt. A sum of 2.4 million yen ($20,000) would get her back on track. In exchange, she promised to cut Terada in on a share of the profits from the business. The money was in her account the next day. The day after, Takao Terada was dead.

Kanae Kijima had thus far managed to commit at least three murders and countless frauds, and yet somehow to fly below police radars. Most of her living victims were embarrassed about being so easily duped, and as for the dead, well, dead men tell no tales. But with her next murder, Kijima would finally overstep the mark, leading to her eventual arrest.

Yoshiyuki Oide was typical of the sort of men that Kijima preyed on. A shy and lonely 41-year-old, Oide's hobby was building model tanks. He kept a blog on which he posted pictures of his creations, usually with a description and history of the vehicle in question. However, on August 2, he oddly broke the pattern to post something personal.

"At 41, I've found someone and I'm going to meet her family, so I may not be able to write as much," he announced. "We're talking about buying a house and starting a new life together. I'll be going on a three-day trip with my fiancée before the wedding."

On 6 August, Oide's corpse was found slumped across the back seat of a rented car in Tokyo's northern suburbs. Beside him lay a charcoal burner, commonly used as a means of suicide in Japan. However, something about the scene did not gel with investigators. For starters, the keys were missing from the ignition. Who had taken them? Then, an autopsy revealed that, although Oide had died of carbon monoxide poisoning, there were traces of a sedative in his bloodstream. Then there was Oide's demeanor in the days leading up to his death. The excited post about his pending marriage did not appear to be the action of someone who was contemplating suicide. Finally, there was motive, 5 million yen ($46,000) removed from the victim's bank account. The police immediately launched a search for Yoshiyuki Oide's mysterious fiancée. It led them eventually to the doorstep of Kanae Kijima's latest conquest, Naoki Yasuda.

Kijima was initially charged with 12 counts of fraud. But the murder of Yoshiyuki Oide was added to the docket after investigators raided Kijima's apartment and found several types of

sedative drug, including the type used to incapacitate Oide. Kijima
was subsequently indicted for two additional murders, those of
Takao Terada and Kenzo Ando.

But the case against Kijima was far from solid. She readily
admitted fraud but denied murder, saying that Ando had died of
natural causes and that Oide and Terada had taken their own lives
after she'd ended her relationships with them. The prosecutor
countered by branding her a serial killer and demanding the death
penalty. After a trial that lasted 100 days, the judge came down on
the side of the prosecution.

On April 13, 2012, Kanae Kijima was found guilty and sentenced to
death. She currently awaits execution.

The case has been widely debated in Japan. In a country where
women still traditionally occupy a subservient role, Kanae Kijima
represents a new kind of monster. And the impact on Japan's
thriving internet dating model has been palpable. "How many
more Kijimas are out there?" one popular blogger wrote. "It's
terrifying."

Ethel Major

It was no secret in Kirkby-on-Bain that Ethel and Arthur Major hated each other. The couple had, after all, carried out a very public spat that had tongues wagging all over the tiny Lincolnshire village. It was Ethel who fired the first salvo. She began spreading stories of her husband's infidelity with a neighbor, tried to have him evicted from the council house they shared and attempted to have him fired from his job as a truck driver, by reporting to the police that he was usually drunk behind the wheel.

Arthur, of course, was not about to take that lying down. He took out an advertisement in the local paper, the Horncastle News, declaring that he would no longer be liable for his wife's debts. He also told anyone who would listen that Ethel was a mean-spirited shrew. He would not have turned to another woman, he said, if he had received even a modicum of kindness at home.

How had it come to this? How had this once happy union devolved into outright warfare between the parties concerned? The answer, as it does in all the best stories, lies in a deep dark secret.

Ethel Lille Brown was born in Lincolnshire in 1891. Her father was a gamekeeper on the estate of Sir Henry Hawley, and Ethel and her three brothers were raised in comfortable surroundings. After leaving school, she was apprenticed to a dressmaker and showed a natural talent for that profession. However, in 1914, aged 22, she became pregnant, a disaster for an unmarried young woman during that era. Seeking to avoid a scandal, her parents brought up the child Auriel as their own and presented her to the world as Ethel's sister.

Four years later, in 1918, Ethel Brown fell for a soldier named Arthur Major, freshly returned from the Great War and with the medals and scars to prove it. Their courtship was short and passionate, leading to a spring wedding on June 1, 1918. The following year, their son Lawrence was born and, in 1929, the family moved to Kirkby-on-Bain.

Contemporary reports as to Ethel's character differ substantially. Some portray her as a decent and serious woman who doted on her son and was a good wife to her husband. Others say that she was cantankerous, ill-tempered and always ready to pick a fight. Whatever the truth, it is safe to say that there were no significant problems in the Majors' marriage until 1934, when Arthur got wind of a vicious rumor regarding his wife's past. The story held that Auriel Brown was not Ethel's younger sister but rather her illicit offspring. Confronted with the allegation, Ethel eventually broke down and confessed, although she refused to provide the name of the child's father when Arthur demanded it.

Thus a breach was opened up between Ethel and Arthur, a gap that would only widen over the ensuing months. Arthur, who had until then been of relatively sober habits, started hitting the bottle and abusing his wife, both verbally and physically. He also began an affair with a neighbor, Rose Kettleborough, something that Ethel discovered when she found a bundle of love letters that had passed between her husband and his mistress. In response, Ethel took to leaving the house each evening, traveling a considerable distance to her parents' home and spending the night there. The marriage, it was clear, had irrevocably broken down.

No one knows for sure when Ethel Major first hatched the plot to poison her husband. The first indication that anything was amiss came on a spring day in 1934, when Arthur sat down with a co-worker to eat his packed lunch. No sooner had he taken a bite into his sandwich when he spat it out, complaining that it tasted bitter. "I swear that woman is trying to poison me," he complained, only half joking.

A couple of months later on May 23, Arthur came home from work feeling unwell and went directly to bed. A doctor was called and arrived to find him sweating, suffering convulsions and unable to talk. Asked about any medical conditions that her husband was prone to, Ethel said that he sometimes suffered fits. She added also that he had consumed some corned beef that day and suggested that the meat might be the reason for his malaise.

The doctor, however, leaned more towards a mild attack of epilepsy. He left after prescribing a sedative and telling Ethel that he would drop by the next day. That, as it turned out, would prove unnecessary. The following morning, Ethel showed up at the doctor's rooms and told him that her husband had died during the night. She also pressed him for a death certificate, saying that she wanted to bury Arthur "as soon as decency permitted."

The death of Arthur Major would likely have passed into history unmarked but for an anonymous letter that arrived at the local police station a day after he died. It read:

"Sir,

Have you ever heard of a wife poisoning her husband? Look further into the death (by heart failure) of Mr. Major of Kirkby-on-Bain. Why did he complain of his food tasting nasty and throw it to a neighbor's dog, which has since died? Ask the undertaker if he looked natural after death. Why did he stiffen so quickly? Why was he so jerky when dying? I myself have heard her threaten to poison him years ago. In the name of the law, I beg you to analyze the contents of his stomach."

The letter was signed, *"Fairplay."*

The police, of course, receive many such tip-offs. Often they are motivated by spite or petty grudges. But in this case, there appeared enough cause for them to obtain a coroner's order postponing the funeral. Then Arthur Major's body was sent to Dr. Roche Lynch at St Mary's Hospital in Paddington, London. It did not take the eminent pathologist long to establish that Arthur had died from strychnine poisoning.

Ethel was brought in for questioning and immediately resorted to the explanation she'd given the doctor. She said that her husband had most likely been poisoned by the corned beef he'd eaten. Asked why she had not been similarly afflicted, she said that she hated the taste of corned beef and never touched the stuff.

Ethel was holding up well under interrogation. But then she made a classic slip up, revealing inside information that only the police and the killer would have been privy to. "I did not give my husband strychnine," she told her interrogator, Chief Inspector Young.

"But madam," Young replied, "I never mentioned strychnine, so how could you know he was given strychnine?"

"Oh, I'm sorry," she replied timidly, "I must have made a mistake."

She had indeed. Their suspicions roused, the police carried out a search of her house. They found nothing incriminating. Then they learned that Ethel often slept over at her parents' home. Again a search turned up no evidence of poison. None, that is, until Young asked Ethel's father directly whether he had any strychnine on the premises. Mr. Brown said that he kept some to kill rodents but insisted that it was locked in a box to which he had the only key. Under further probing, he admitted that there had been a second key but said that it had been lost some ten years previously. That missing key would eventually be found in the Major residence when the police searched it for a second time.

Ethel Major was brought before the Lincoln Assizes on October 29, 1934, her case attracting so much interest that villagers from Kirkby-on-Bain hired a bus to travel to the trial. She was defended by the renowned barrister, Mr. Norman Birkett, who had, to that point, never lost a single murder case in his long and distinguished career. But not even Birkett could come up with a defense strategy for a client who had so recklessly incriminated herself. It took the jury less than an hour to reach its verdict. Ethel had to be carried into the dock to hear the judge pronounce penalty of death. She immediately collapsed on hearing the sentence.

Yet few had any taste for seeing a woman put to death on the gallows. The jury had recommended mercy, and the Lord Mayor of Hull even petitioned King George V directly, asking him to intervene. In the end, it did no good. The Home Secretary, Sir John Gilmour, refused to commute the sentence, and Ethel Major kept her date with the hangman on Wednesday, December 19, 1934. She was the first woman put to death at Hull Goal. Her ghost is said to haunt the prison to this day.

Theresa Cross

On the morning of July 17, 1984, detectives from Tahoe City, California, were summoned to a grisly murder scene. A motorist had been driving along Highway 89 when she spotted a small fire in the woods close to the road. Summoning the help of another driver, she'd gone to investigate and had made a horrific discovery: a charred human corpse burning in the undergrowth.

The body was that of a young female, later estimated by the medical examiner to be between 18 and 22 years old. It was quite obvious that she had met with foul play, but detectives would only appreciate the full, horrific extent of the crime once the M.E. completed his work. The young woman's injuries suggested that she had suffered severe physical abuse over an extended period. Worse still, she'd still been alive when she'd been doused with gasoline and set on fire. She had died of smoke inhalation.

With little chance of identifying the victim, she was named Jane Doe #4873/84. Jane's fingers were removed and sent to Sacramento for fingerprinting, while her upper and lower jawbones were also removed and placed in storage, in case dental records later became available for comparison. However, investigators held out very little hope of solving the case. It would remain unresolved for nearly a decade before the horrendous truth would emerge. Jane Doe was Susan Marlene Knorr. Her killer was her own mother, a human monster by the name of Theresa Jimmie Cross.

Theresa Jimmie Francine Cross was born on March 12, 1946, in Sacramento, California. Her father, Jim Cross, was a cheese maker at Golden State Dairy, while her mother, Swannie Gay Cross, worked for a local lumber company. Theresa had an older sister, Rosemary, and two older step-siblings, William and Clara.

The family prospered over the years, and by the early 1950s, they were able to move into a large house in Rio Linda, California. But their happiness was short-lived. During the late '50s, Jim Cross developed Parkinson's disease and was forced to quit his job. Thereafter he suffered from depression and became increasingly irritable, taking out his frustrations on his children.

As a child, Theresa was a loner, who clashed constantly with her sister, Rosemary, usually over the attentions of their mother. Theresa was particularly close to her mother, so when Swannie Cross collapsed and died during a shopping trip on March 2, 1961, it hit her hard. Those who knew Theresa said that she was never the same after that.

Following her mother's death, Theresa fell into a deep depression. But there was worse to come. Without Swannie's income, Jim

Cross could no longer afford to keep the family home and was forced to sell it. Other family assets went the same way as the security Theresa had taken for granted was eroded bit by bit. Desperate for a way out, she found it in the form of Clifford Clyde Sanders.

Theresa first met Cliff, five years her senior, at the home of a mutual friend. They were instantly attracted to each other and, within weeks, Cliff had popped the question. Desperate to escape her home life, Theresa said yes. They married on September 29, 1962. Shortly thereafter, Theresa dropped out of junior high and moved with her husband to a one-bedroom apartment in North Highlands.

On July 16, 1963, Theresa gave birth to their first child, Howard Clyde Sanders. But by then, the marriage was already in trouble. Theresa was exceedingly possessive and liked to keep her husband on a short leash. Clifford responded by staying away from the family home and going out drinking with his buddies, something that always resulted in a blazing row when he returned home.

Matters eventually came to a head on July 5, 1964. Cliff had been out drinking as usual and arrived home to a raging Theresa. She accused him of infidelity, and Cliff finally decided that enough was enough. The following morning, he packed a bag and told Theresa he was leaving her. He never made it through the door. In a rage, Theresa grabbed a rifle and shot him dead.

By the time the police arrived, Theresa had her story all worked out. She said that they had argued the previous evening over Cliff's drinking and that the argument had picked up again in the morning. Then things had gotten physical and Cliff had struck her. She had picked up the rifle to defend herself and it had accidentally discharged, hitting him in the heart.

To detectives, the story had the ring of truth to it, especially as Theresa had filed assault charges against her husband just weeks before. However, the D.A. decided differently and charged Theresa with murder. At her trial, in August 1964, Theresa entered a self-defense plea, and the jury agreed with her. On September 22, after deliberating for just one hour and 45 minutes, they returned a verdict of not guilty. Just 18 years old and pregnant with her second child, the widow Sanders walked away a free woman.

Following her acquittal, Theresa regained custody of her son Howard and moved in with family friends. Lonely and desperately seeking some stability in her life, she began drowning her sorrows at a local American Legion Hall. It was there that she met and started dating Lee Thornsberry, an Army vet who was confined to a wheelchair after a swimming accident left him a quadriplegic.

On March 13, 1965, Theresa gave birth to a daughter, Sheila Gay Sanders. Even though the child was not his, Thornsberry doted on the little girl. When he suggested that Theresa and the children move in with him, she happily agreed. However, the blissful arrangement did not last long. It soon became clear to Thornsberry that Theresa was using him as a glorified babysitter, there to watch over the children while she went out drinking. Within a few months, he also learned that Theresa was sleeping with one of his buddies. After one argument too many, Theresa packed her belongings and moved out.

But the attractive, young mother would not be without company for long. Her next conquest was another military man, Marine Corps private Robert Knorr. A few months after they started dating, Theresa was pregnant, and they began discussing marriage.

In February 1966, those plans were put on hold when Knorr was shipped off to Vietnam. His tour of duty would be a short one. After sustaining serious injuries in an explosion, he returned to the US where he spent several months recovering at Oakland Naval Hospital. After his discharge, he and Theresa drove to Nevada and exchanged vows in front of a local judge. Two months later, on September 27, 1966, Theresa gave birth to her third child, a girl who she named Susan Marlene Knorr. A fourth child arrived barely a year later, on September 15, 1967. He was named William Robert Knorr. And Theresa's fifth child, another boy, was born on December 31, 1968. Theresa named him Robert Wallace Knorr.

Things appeared to be going well for the Knorrs. But as always with Theresa, trouble wasn't far away. She began to resent Robert's new job, which involved him traveling around the country as a burial escort for the military. Tempers often flared and, as she'd done with Clifford Sanders, she began accusing Robert of infidelity. She had also found a new outlet for her ire – her children. She would force them to sit on the floor without moving, delivering a swift slap to any child who so much as batted an eye. If that didn't work, she would lock them in a closet or, alternatively, force-feed them until they threw up.

By June 1970, the Knorrs' marriage had deteriorated to the point where both parties agreed to a divorce. Two months later, Theresa gave birth to her sixth child, a daughter named Theresa Marie Knorr. In 1971, she married a man named Ronald Pulliam, but that marriage followed an all too familiar path and ended in divorce just over a year later. Unperturbed by her failures in love, Theresa tied the knot again in August 1976, this time with 59-year-old Chet Harris. This marriage, Theresa's last, was over in just three months. Shortly thereafter, she reverted to her maiden name – Theresa Jimmie Cross.

Following her latest divorce, Theresa started drinking heavily and putting on weight. She also became a recluse, barely leaving the house and even disconnecting the telephone because she didn't want anyone calling her. And her abuse of her children also started to escalate. On one occasion, she took to throwing steak knives at them. On another, she held a .22-caliber pistol to the head of her youngest child, Terry. Then there were the beatings, during which she'd force the other children to hold down one of their siblings while she punched and slapped the helpless child.

Theresa liked to refer to her children as "demon seeds given to me by Bob Knorr," but no one suspected that she meant it literally. At one point, she became convinced that her daughter Susan was a witch. As a result, Susan began to bear the brunt of her mother's physical abuse. After one particularly brutal beating, the terrified girl ran away from home, only to be returned by a truancy officer. That resulted in one of the most severe beatings Susan had ever received, with her siblings forced to participate in doling out the punishment. Thereafter, Susan was chained to a bed frame at night to prevent her from escaping again. Her mother also withdrew her from school.

But even with Susan entirely under her control, Theresa continued to believe that the girl was using magical powers to harm her. She accused Susan of casting a spell that was causing her to gain weight. All of Susan's denials fell on deaf ears as Theresa flew into a rage, picked up her .22-caliber pistol and fired. Susan collapsed to the floor with blood pumping from a chest wound. As she writhed in pain, Theresa ordered the other children to carry her to the bathroom and place her in the tub.

Calling an ambulance was out of the question, as the matter would then have to be reported to the police. Instead, Theresa decided that she would remove the bullet herself. However, it had penetrated so deep that removal proved impossible. Theresa, therefore, decided to leave the slug embedded in her daughter's flesh. The wound was covered over with gauze and bandages, and over the months that followed, Susan gradually recovered from her injury. During that time, she was at least spared from the regular beatings.

But the truce did not last long. In November 1983, Theresa got into a heated argument with Susan, during which she stabbed her daughter in the back with a pair of scissors. The wound was not life-threatening, but Susan had finally had enough. She told her mother that she was moving out and, surprisingly, Theresa agreed. There was one stipulation. Theresa wanted to remove the bullet that remained lodged in her daughter's back. She didn't want that coming back to her if Susan decided to go to the police. Left with little other option, Susan agreed.

The crude operation was carried out a few days later. In lieu of anesthetic, Susan was given a handful of painkillers, to be washed down with vodka. Theresa's son Robert was coerced into doing the cutting, using an X-Acto knife as a scalpel. Amazingly, he was able to locate the slug, embedded deep in the muscles of his sister's back.

But if the operation was a qualified success, the recovery was not. Susan woke from her ordeal in extreme pain. Within days, the whites of her eyes had turned a sickly shade of yellow, and she'd lost control of her bowels. Dark blotches began to appear on her back, indicative of internal bleeding.

On July 16, 1984, with Susan in a near comatose state, Theresa decided to act. First, she packed up all of Susan's belongings in black trash bags. Then she placed duct tape over Susan's mouth and tied her arms and legs. Finally, she instructed Robert and William to carry Susan and her things out to the car. Also on board was a canister of gasoline which Theresa personally loaded into the trunk.

They headed south on Highway 89, eventually leaving the road at Square Creek Bridge. Just into the trees, Bill and Robert were ordered to take Susan out of the car and carry her down to the creek bank. Theresa brought down the garbage bags and placed them beside Susan. She then doused everything with gasoline and struck a match. She and her sons drove away while Susan was burning to death.

In the spring of 1985, Theresa decided to supplement her small state income by sending out her 20-year-old daughter Sheila to work the streets as a prostitute. Sheila was horrified by the idea, but she knew better than to challenge her mother's authority. Before long, she was bringing home hundreds of dollars a day, something that pleased Theresa and earned Sheila a reprieve from the regular beatings. But it did not last long.

In May 1985, Theresa began to suspect that her daughter was pregnant and also accused her of having a venereal disease. Sheila denied these allegations, but that only earned her a harsh beating. She was then hog-tied and locked in a tiny bathroom closet. Sheila was left without food and water in the stiflingly hot space. She was told that she could leave only if she confessed her transgression. Yet when Sheila did admit that she had a sexually transmitted disease, it earned her no respite. Her mother now claimed that she was lying simply to gain her freedom.

Sheila remained locked in the closet without food and water for six days. On June 24, Theresa opened the closet door and found her daughter's already decomposing body. She immediately ordered her sons to fetch a cardboard box and load their sister's remains into the car. They then headed up Interstate 80 and dumped the corpse in a small field near Truckee Airport. It was discovered a few hours later. With no way to identify the body, Sheila entered the record books as another Jane Doe.

Theresa became extremely paranoid after Sheila's death, convinced that the closet contained evidence that could implicate her in the crime. On September 29, 1986, she decided to cut and run. Packing up all of the family's belongings, she doused the house with lighter fluid and set it alight. However, neighbors soon noticed the blaze and called the fire department. They arrived to put out the fire before the house sustained any serious damage. By then, Theresa Cross and her clan were long gone.

But by now Theresa was losing control of her children. One by one, they began drifting away until only Robert remained with his mother. They fled to Las Vegas and remained under the radar until November 1991, when Robert walked into a bar on North Nellis Boulevard and pulled out a gun. His intention was to rob the place, but the bartender offered resistance and Robert shot him. Tried for second-degree murder, he was sentenced to 16 years in jail. Nervous at the attention his trial garnered, Theresa left town and moved to Salt Lake City, Utah. She might well have escaped justice but for another tweak of fate in this already convoluted case.

In 1992, Theresa's youngest daughter, Terry, was watching an episode of America's Most Wanted when she was suddenly overcome with the urge to seek justice for her murdered sisters. She decided to call the Sheriff's office in Nevada County, California, where Sergeant Ron Perea listened with interest to her wild tale and then asked if he could meet her in person. An interview was set up for the following day. After speaking to Terry for several hours, Perea took his notes to the D.A., and a task force was assembled to check out Terry's claims. It didn't take long to tie in the two Jane Doe reports to the story.

On November 4, 1993, investigators filed felony complaints against Theresa and two of her sons. William was traced to a Sacramento suburb, while Robert was easy to find. He was serving time in Nevada County jail. Five days later, Theresa was tracked to

Utah, where she'd recently been arrested on a drunk driving charge. Investigators arrived at her door just in time. Inside were packed suitcases. She had been about to flee the jurisdiction.

With both of her sons admitting to their parts in the murders and striking a deal with prosecutors, there was never a chance that Theresa Cross would escape justice. Still, she continued to maintain her innocence until it became clear that the D.A. intended seeking the death penalty. Then she asked for a deal of her own, a guilty plea in exchange for life in prison. District Attorney John O'Mara agreed, and on October 17, 1995, Theresa was sentenced to two consecutive life terms. She will be eligible for parole in 2027, by which time she will be 80 years old.

Caroline Grills

Caroline Grills makes a most unlikely serial killer. For starters, she was 63 years old at the time of her arrest. Secondly, she was everyone's favorite aunt, always visiting with home-baked cakes and cookies, always ready to put the kettle on for a nice cup of tea. Still, people did have a nasty habit of dying when "Aunty Carrie" was around, and a relative eventually got suspicious. After spotting her slipping something into his tea, he furtively poured some of the liquid into a bottle, which he later handed over to the police. It was tested and found to contain copious amounts of thallium, a substance commonly found in rat poison during that era.

Caroline Grills (nee Mickelson) was born in Balmain, a suburb of Sydney, Australia, in 1888, the daughter of a laborer named George Mickelson and his wife Mary. She grew up to be a squat, somewhat homely girl who appeared no different to her peers in temperament or habits. Married to a laborer named Richard Grills at age 20, she would go on to deliver six children, five boys and a girl. Two of the boys would die tragically in adolescence, one of

them from typhoid, contracted while working as a lifesaver at
Maroubra beach.

The Grills family seems to have had a fairly nomadic existence,
living in a succession of rented houses in the Randwick area until
1948, when Caroline's father died and she inherited his property
in Gladesville. By then, Caroline was a dumpy 60-year-old who
wore thick glasses and walked with an odd waddle. She was,
however, well-loved, especially by her in-laws who she visited
often. On those occasions she usually arrived bearing gifts: cakes
and cookies that she'd baked in her kitchen. Aunt Carrie, everyone
agreed, was an excellent baker.

But then there were the suspicious deaths, the first of these
occurring in November 1947. Christina Mickelson, Caroline's
stepmother, was a healthy, robust woman, with whom Caroline
had a good relationship. The two could often be found nattering
together over a cup of tea, enjoying some of Caroline's excellent
cookies. Despite her advanced age, it was a surprise to everyone
when Christina started having health problems, particularly
problems that manifested in such unusual ways. First, her hair
started falling out, coming away from her scalp in clumps. Then
she developed an odd nervous tic and started to complain of
blurred vision. Finally, she suffered weakness in her legs and lost
the power of speech. She died at home, with Caroline by her
bedside. Death, when it came, must have felt like a mercy.

Although nobody knew it at the time, Christina Mickelson had
displayed the classic signs of thallium poisoning. And she was but
the first of Caroline's immediate circle to suffer these agonies. In
January 1948, Angelina Thomas, an aunt of Caroline's husband,

died of symptoms that were remarkably similar. Then, in late 1948, it was the turn of her husband's brother-in-law, John Lundberg. He was followed to the grave by a friend of Caroline's stepmother, another who had consumed one of Caroline's confections.

Throughout 1951 and 1952, several of Caroline's family became ill, all with the now familiar indicators. Eveline Lundberg and her daughter, Christine Downey were particularly afflicted, suffering several bouts of the mystery ailment. It was Christine's husband, John, who first noticed that the women's symptoms always seemed to arise after a visit from Aunty Carrie, and that they recovered whenever Caroline had not been to visit for a few days. It was he who laid the trap, he who held back the poisoned tea and took it to the police. Grills was then brought in for questioning but denied poisoning anyone. Those denials, however, would prove to be a lie, after autopsies were conducted on the exhumed bodies of her suspected victims. Two of the corpses showed clear signs of thallium poisoning.

Caroline Grills was brought before a coroner's inquest, where several family members testified as to how Caroline always arrived with baked goods and how she always insisted on making the tea. John Downey described how he'd seen Grills slipping something into his cup and how he'd saved the liquid and taken it to the police. Eveline Lundberg even got up from her sickbed to testify as to her horrific symptoms. Add to that the results of the autopsies and the tests conducted on the tainted tea, and it came as no surprise when Grills was indicted. She was charged with the murders of Mary Anne Mickelson, Christina Louisa Mickelson, and Angelina Thomas. She was also charged with the attempted murders of several of her relatives, including Eveline Lundberg.

By the time the matter came to trial, however, the state prosecutor had decided to drop all of the murder charges. Since no one had actually seen Grills giving poison to her victims, the prosecutor felt that the cases would be impossible to prove. There was, however, still a case to answer for the attempted murder of Mrs. Eveline Lundberg. Grills vigorously denied this charge, but her behavior in court, particularly her disconcerting habit of laughing whenever there was a particularly macabre revelation, suggested otherwise. Perhaps she really was what Senior Crown Prosecutor Mick Rooney described her as: "A killer who poisoned for sport, for fun, for the kicks she got out of it, for the hell of it, for the thrill that she and she alone in the world knew the cause of the victims' suffering."

The jury seemed to agree with Rooney's assessment, taking just twelve minutes to reach its decision. On October 15, 1953, Caroline Grills was found guilty of attempted murder and sentenced to death.

Grills's attorney appealed of course, but the petition was dismissed by the Court of Criminal Appeal. Then, just when it appeared that the deadly granny would swing for her crimes, the Governor-General commuted the sentence to life imprisonment. Grills was sent to the State Reformatory for Women at Sydney's Long Bay Prison, where she would spend the last six-and-a-half years of her life.

Grills was a popular inmate, known affectionately to other inmates as "Aunty Thally." There was genuine sadness at the prison when she died on October 6, 1960, as the result of a ruptured ulcer. She remains an enigma in the annals of Australian crime, her motives unknown. Her crimes did, however, have one positive effect. Soon after her conviction, the sale of thallium was banned in the Commonwealth of Australia.

Dorothea Puente

The stench hanging over the quiet, tree-lined Sacramento neighborhood was overpowering. Everyone knew where it was coming from - the pale blue two-story Victorian house at number 1426 F Street, where Dorothea Puente ran a boarding house for the elderly and infirm. Puente offered any number of explanations for the reek, insisting that "the sewer's backed up" or "it's the fish emulsion I used to fertilize the garden or "rats have died under the floorboards." She also spent an inordinate amount of time trying to disguise the smell, using bags of lime and gallons of bleach in the yard and spraying her parlor several times a day with lemon-scented air freshener. Still the stink persisted, hanging over the boardinghouse like a fetid mist.

Yet, when the police arrived at number 1426, it wasn't in response to complaints from neighbors, but to search for one of Mrs. Puente's tenants, who had mysteriously disappeared. Four days earlier, on November 7, a social worker named Judy Moise had filed a missing persons report on Alvaro "Bert" Montoya, a mentally retarded man whom Moise had placed with Puente.

Puente insisted that Bert had gone to Mexico, but Moise didn't believe her. Officers therefore went to the house to question Puente. While they were there, one of the other tenants handed them a note, describing how Puente had lied about Montoya's disappearance. It was enough for police to obtain a search warrant for the house and garden.

On the morning of November 11, 1988, Detective John Cabrera arrived at number 1426 and presented Dorothy Puente with his warrant. "Go ahead," she said when Cabrera asked if the police could begin their search.

Despite the cloying stench, the interior was scrupulously clean, lace curtains in the windows, doilies decorating the tables, vases, porcelain dolls and other knickknacks everywhere. Nothing seemed out of the ordinary. The yard, though, was another story. At the southeast corner of the property, the ground had been recently disturbed. That looked suspicious, so Cabrera sent officers to fetch shovels to evacuate the area.

Just a couple of feet down, they turned up shreds of cloth and what appeared to be chunks of desiccated flesh. Then, when their efforts were thwarted by what looked like a tree root, one of the officers got into the hole and tried to dislodge it. The "root" came loose in his hands and to his horror turned out to be a human leg bone. Cabrera then stopped the search and called in a crime scene unit.

The next morning, a team of forensic anthropologists and coroner's officers arrived at the property with a county work crew.

They soon found the first body, a frail female with gray hair still rooted in her skull.

A crowd of onlookers had by now gathered to watch the proceedings from the other side of the high fence. Soon the crowd was supplemented by TV crews and newspaper reporters. Kids scaled trees for a better look, while camera crews climbed onto the roofs of their vans. The atmosphere was that of a street party, but that would soon change as the bodies started to come out.

As the work crew started drilling through a slab of concrete and prepared to excavate beneath it, Dorothy Puente walked into the yard. She was dressed to the nines, a cherry red overcoat, purple pumps, and a pink umbrella, her makeup immaculately applied. She asked Detective Cabrera if she was under arrest. When he said "No," she asked if she could go to the nearby Clarion Hotel for a cup of coffee. Cabrera said that would be okay, even arranging for officers to escort her through the crowd of onlookers.

Three more bodies turned up under the concrete slab, while another was discovered under the gazebo. That brought the total to five. By the time the search ended, another four hours had passed and another two bodies had been discovered. It was then that Cabrera realized that Dorothea Puente hadn't returned from the hotel. By then, she was already hundreds of miles away.

Dorothea Puente was born Dorothea Helen Gray on January 9, 1929, in Redlands, California. Her parents, Jesse James Gray and Trudy Mae Yates, were cotton-pickers who spent most of their meager wages on booze, leaving their six children poorly clothed and unfed. When Dorothea was four, her father died of tuberculosis. Just over a year later her mother followed him to the grave courtesy of a motorcycle accident. Orphaned at six, Dorothea became a ward of the state until relatives in Fresno, California, took her in.

School records show that she was a student in Los Angeles in 1945, but less than a year later, she moved to Olympia, Washington, where she found work in a milkshake parlor.

In 1946, she met Fred McFaul, a 22-year-old solider just back from the war, and the two were soon married. McFaul quickly learned that his 16-year-old bride knew how to use her good looks to get what she wanted (there are suggestions she was working as a prostitute when he met her). He also found out that she was an inveterate liar. She claimed to have lived through the Bataan Death March and the bombing of Hiroshima, she said she was the sister of the ambassador to Sweden, and a close friend of Rita Hayworth.

McFaul and Puente set up house in Gardnerville, Nevada, but shortly after the birth of the couple's second daughter, Puente left for Los Angeles. She returned several months later, pregnant with another man's child. She miscarried the baby, but McFaul left her anyway. The couple's daughters were later adopted.

Left to her own devices, Puente fell into a life of petty crime, resulting eventually in her arrest for forgery in 1948. She served four years in prison, then skipped out on her parole after her release.

In 1952, she married her second husband, a Swedish merchant seaman named Axel Johansson. They would remain together for 14 years, but the marriage was turbulent, characterized by violent clashes, break-ups and reconciliations. Johansson would often return from his trips abroad to find other men living with his wife. Neighbors complained about taxis dropping off men at all hours of the night.

In 1960, Puente was arrested for living in a brothel. She claimed she was only visiting a friend and didn't know it was a house of ill repute. Still she was given 90 days in Sacramento County Jail. A charge of vagrancy following her release landed her with another 90 days.

Although still legally married to Axel Johansson, he provided her with no financial support, leaving Puente to fend for herself. She did so the only way she knew how, through petty larcenies. She might well have ended up back in prison had she not discovered a legitimate way to earn a living. She became a nurse's aide, caring for the disabled and elderly. Soon after, she began managing boarding houses.

In 1966, Puente divorced Johansson and married Robert Puente in Mexico City. Roberto was nineteen years her junior and by all accounts quite the lothario. His constant dalliances eventually got to Dorothea, and the couple divorced after two years. At around this time, Dorothea began managing a three-story, sixteen-bedroom care home at 2100 F Street. For all her other shortcomings, Puente was an excellent hostess and the house thrived under her proprietorship. A stern landlady who ran a tight ship, Puente was valued by local social workers because she was prepared to take on problem tenants who no one else would accommodate.

In 1976, Puente married for the third time. Her new husband, Pedro Montalvo, was a physically abusive alcoholic, and the marriage was short-lived. Within months, Montalvo was gone and Puente took to seeking out male company in local dives. She was still fairly attractive, a sharp dresser and a pleasant companion, and the older men she targeted were drawn to her. Puente's method was simple. She'd charm her way into her victim's lives, then steal their benefit checks and cash them. The scheme worked for a while, but it was always going to catch up with her. When it did, she was charged with 34 counts of treasury fraud. She received five years' probation and was ordered to undergo counseling. A psychiatrist who interviewed her at the time diagnosed her as a schizophrenic and a "very disturbed woman."

In the spring of 1982, Puente committed her first murder, although at the time the death of 61-year-old Ruth Munroe was ruled a suicide. Puente and Munroe were business partners in a small lunchroom business, and Munroe moved into Puente's boarding house, bringing her life's savings of $6,000 in cash. Two weeks later, she was dead of a massive overdose of Tylenol and codeine. Puente said that Munroe had been depressed because her husband was terminally ill and confined to a VA Hospital. The coroner accepted her story and ruled that Munroe had taken her own life.

A month later, Puente was arrested on a separate charge. She was accused of drugging four elderly men and stealing their valuables. One of the victims, a 74-year-old-man, told police that Puente had doped him, then looted his home, taking his rare coin collection and even forcing a diamond ring from his finger as he sat paralyzed, unable to move or speak.

On August 18, 1982, Puente appeared before a judge and was convicted on three charges of theft and sentenced to five years imprisonment.

Puente had done time before and she quickly adapted to prison life. She also acquired a pen pal, a 77-year-old retiree named Everson Gillmouth who made a habit of writing to female inmates. Before long Puente's words had charmed Gillmouth to such an extent that he declared his love. When she was released in September 1985, he was waiting for her in his red 1980 Ford pickup.

The relationship between Puente and Gillmouth developed quickly. Before long, he'd opened a joint banking account and the couple were talking marriage. Puente had meanwhile found lodgings at a boarding house on F Street run by her old friend Ricardo Odorica. Not long after moving in, Puente offered Odorica $600 a month to rent the whole house. He agreed, and her dream of running a boarding house again had become a reality.

In November 1985, Puente hired a local handyman, Ismael Florez, to put up some wood paneling in her house, offering him a red 1980 Ford pickup in payment. She added one odd request. She wanted Florez to build her a box, 6 feet long, 3 feet wide and 2 feet deep. She needed it, she said, to store some books and other odds. If Florez wondered about the strange dimensions, he never asked.

The following day when he returned to the job, the box had been filled and nailed shut. Puente then asked if he'd help her transport the box to the storage depot and Florez agreed. However, they never made it that far. On the way to the depot, Puente suddenly changed her mind and instructed Florez to dump the box on a riverbank. It contained mainly junk anyway, she said.

On New Year's Day, 1986, a couple of fishermen found the box half-submerged in water. They informed the police, who pried the lid open and discovered the severely decomposed remains of Everson Gillmouth. Unable to identify the corpse, he was listed as a "John Doe" and would remain so for the next three years. During that time, Puente continued to collect his pension and wrote letters to his family, blaming his lack of contact on ill health.

Puente by now had a full roster of tenants in her boarding house, many of them alcoholics and drug addicts. She was making good money and squandering it all on a lavish lifestyle of expensive clothes, perfume, even plastic surgery. Puente's method at this time was to collect all of her tenants' mail, take control of their benefit checks and pay them only a small allowance. Usually, this money would be blown on booze at the nearest bar. Puente would then make an anonymous call reporting them drunk and disorderly. That would earn them 30 days in the slammer, during which time Puente would pocket their benefit money.

Somewhere along the line, Puente must have hit on the idea of making them disappear for good. In the following months, a number of mysterious disappearances were reported. On August 19, Betty Palmer, a 77-year-old resident of Puente's boarding house, went to the doctor and never returned. In February the following year, another tenant, Leona Carpenter, 78, was placed in Puente's care. Two weeks later, she was gone, never to be heard from again.

James Gallop was 62 when he disappeared in July 1987, not long after moving into 1426 F Street. In October, Vera Martin, 62, also vanished after moving into the boarding house.

And then there was Bert Montoya, whose disappearance would ultimately bring about Puente's downfall. Puente told the other tenants that Bert had gone to Mexico to visit his family, something they found difficult to swallow as they knew Bert was from Costa Rica.

Even before Montoya's disappearance, Puente had begun to arouse suspicion. A Department of Social Services inspector had visited Puente's boarding house to investigate a report that she'd misused her tenants' benefits. The inspector declared the complaints unfounded.

A social worker named Peggy Nickerson had also became suspicious of the number of people who had gone missing from Puente's care. Puente told her that they had moved away, which seemed viable given that many of them were transients. Still, Nickerson stopped sending cases to Puente.

Finally, on November 7, Judy Moise had filed the missing persons report on Bert Montoya, bringing Puente's little murder-for-profit enterprise to an abrupt halt.

The police now had seven bodies, all of them showing large concentrations of the drug Dalmane. They were also looking into the disappearance of Everson Gillmouth and the apparent suicide of Ruth Munroe. They had proof that Puente had cashed over 60 benefit checks belonging to the deceased. What they didn't have was Dorothy Puente, who was at that moment safely ensconced in room 31 of the Royal Viking Hotel in downtown Los Angeles.

Having booked in under the name Dorothea Johansson, Puente laid low in her room for a number of days. Eventually, though, she became restless and ventured out, finding her way to a seedy bar some two miles from her hotel.

Charles Willgues, a 59-year-old retiree, was nursing a mid-afternoon beer when a well-dressed stranger took a stool next to him. She ordered a vodka and orange juice, and the two soon struck up a conversation, Puente introducing herself as Donna Johansson. She told Willgues that she was from Sacramento and that her husband had died a month earlier. She also said that when she'd checked into her hotel, the cabbie had driven off with her suitcases. To make matters worse, she'd just broken the heel on her only pair of shoes.

"Donna" must have made quite an impression on Willgues because he immediately took the shoe to a repair shop over the road and had it fixed. When he returned, he and Donna continued their conversation during the course of which she asked him how much money he got from Social Security. Willagues told her he got $576 a month, and Donna then explained to him how he could get more. She seemed very knowledgeable, and he was impressed.

He shirked, though, when the stranger suddenly suggested that they move in together. She was a good cook, she said, and they were two lonely souls in the world, so why shouldn't they keep each other company?

Willgues quickly changed the subject and they had another drink, then left and had a chicken dinner together at a fast food place. In the early evening they parted but made plans to meet up the following day. Yet, even as he walked away, Willgues had the strong feeling that he'd seen Donna somewhere before.

Back at his apartment, Willgues suddenly realized who she was. He'd seen her on TV. She was the woman wanted by police in connection with the bodies found at that Sacramento boarding house. Still, Willgues couldn't bring himself to turn his new acquaintance in to the police. Instead, he called a local TV station, and they passed the tip on to the authorities. "I'm just very thankful that the relationship didn't go any further," Willgues later told reporters.

At 10:40 p.m., LAPD officers arrived at the Royal Viking Hotel and took Puente into custody. She was returned to Sacramento on a flight chartered by KCRA-TV and The Sacramento Bee. During the journey, she told a reporter – "I cashed checks, yes, but I never killed anyone - I used to be a good person once."

Dorothy Puente's trial began in Monterey, California, on February 9, 1993, Judge Michael J. Virga presiding. She stood accused of nine murders, to which her defense team entered not guilty pleas. On

July 15, 1993, having heard 153 witnesses, the jury retired to consider their verdict. On August 2, they informed the judge that they were hopelessly deadlocked.

The following day, ignoring defense motions for a mistrial, Judge Virga sent them back to try again. On the afternoon of August 26, they announced that they had reached a verdict. They found Puente guilty of the second-degree murder of Leona Carpenter, and the first-degree murders of Dorothy Miller and Ben Fink. They were still deadlocked on the other counts, and the judge was forced to declare a mistrial in those cases.

On December 11, 1993, Puente was sentenced to life in prison without the possibility of parole. She was incarcerated at Central California Women's Facility in Chowchilla. She died there of natural causes on March 27, 2011. She was 82 years old.

For more True Crime books by Robert Keller please visit

http://bit.ly/kellerbooks

33553204R00081

Printed in Great Britain
by Amazon